Know Where You're Going

KNOW WHERE YOU'RE GOING

A COMPLETE BUDDHIST GUIDE
TO MEDITATION, FAITH, AND
EVERYDAY TRANSCENDENCE

AYYA KHEMA

WISDOM PUBLICATIONS • BOSTON

Wisdom Publications
199 Elm Street
Somerville, MA 02144 USA
www.wisdompubs.org

Library of Congress Cataloging-in-Publication Data
Khema, Ayya, author.
  [When the iron eagle flies]
  Know where you're going : a complete Buddhist guide to meditation, faith and everyday transcen-
dence / Ayya Khema.
      pages cm
  Originally published: When the iron eagle flies : Boston : Wisdom Publications, 2000.
  Includes bibliographical references and index.
  ISBN 978-1-61429-193-0 — ISBN 1-61429-193-4 (pbk. : alk. paper) — ISBN 978-1-61429-210-4
(eBook)
  1. Buddhism—Doctrines. 2. Meditation—Buddhism. I. Title.
  BQ4165.K485 2014
  294.3'444—dc23

                         2014015481

ISBN 978-1-61429-193-0   Ebook ISBN 978-1-61429-210-4

18 17 16 15 14
5 4 3 2 1

Cover photo "Way to Paradise" by Kilian Schönberger, www.kilianschoenberger.de.
Cover design by Philip Pascuzzo. Interior design by Gopa&Ted2, Inc.
Set in Garamond Premier Pro 11.5/14.56.

Wisdom Publications' books are printed on acid-free paper and meet
the guidelines for permanence and durability of the Production Guidelines
for Book Longevity of the Council on Library Resources.

This book was produced with environmental mindfulness. We have elected to print this title on 30% PCW
recycled paper. As a result, we have saved the following resources: 11 trees, 5 million BTUs of energy, 994
lbs. of greenhouse gases, 5,394 gallons of water, and 361 lbs. of solid waste. For more information, please
visit our website, www.wisdompubs.org.

Printed in the United States of America

MIX
Paper from
responsible sources
FSC
www.fsc.org   FSC® C011935

Please visit www.fscus.org.

Contents

❧ Foreword

AFTER HIS ATTAINMENT of enlightenment the Lord Buddha taught for many years in north India. He counseled his listeners not simply to accept his words out of faith but to think about them and then, if they found them convincing and appropriate, to put the advice into practice. Thus, his teachings spread because they impressed people, who found them useful in their own lives, and in turn passed them on to others. With time Buddhism spread throughout Asia.

However, the relevance of the Buddha's message is not confined to one geographical area, for all human beings can apply what he taught. In recent years people from Western lands have had greater access to living Buddhist tradition and have taken increasing interest in it; some have even become Buddhists themselves. One such is Ayya Khema, who presents here the advice she has given while leading a meditation course in Canada based on her own experience. Such efforts are indeed heartening, and I hope that through them all beings may find peace.

Tenzin Gyatso
H. H. the Fourteenth Dalai Lama

Acknowledgments

THIS BOOK IS DEDICATED to my parents, all my teachers, all my students, all my friends, and all those who have supported the Buddha's teachings in the past and who support them now.

Special thanks come from my heart to the Venerable Pema Chödrön, who invited me to give these teachings, to Ani Trime Lhamo, who transcribed the cassettes on which this book is based, and to Claudia Klump, who diligently helped with the typing.

May beings everywhere rejoice and benefit from these words.

Ayya Khema
Buddha-Haus,
Germany, September 1989

❧ Introduction

BEFORE I BEGIN MY TEACHING I would like to explain the origin of the Buddha's discourses. Three months after the Buddha's death (*parinibbāna*) the first great council of enlightened ones (*arahants*) took place. At that time the Buddha's teaching was systematized and put into orderly categories. When he was alive, he taught as befitted the occasion, often in answer to questions. In those days religious teaching was always transmitted orally.

At the first great council of enlightened ones, the Venerable Ananda, who had been the Buddha's attendant for twenty-five years, recited the discourses (*sutta*s), and the Venerable Upāli recited the Vinaya (the rules of the order of monks and nuns). Approximately 17,500 discourses of the Buddha were thus transmitted. About a hundred years later the second council of enlightened ones was convened. The enlightened ones were called together because there were significant differences of opinion, particularly concerning the Vinaya, and in holding these different viewpoints the Sangha (community of monks and nuns) had split into various factions. It had become imperative to finalize the whole of the Buddha's transmission so that a definitive body of teaching would be safeguarded.

Two hundred and fifty years after the Buddha's *parinibbāna* the third great council of enlightened ones took place. At that time the Venerable Ananda, the Venerable Moggallāna, and the Venerable Sariputta, who had been the great disciples of the Buddha, each had one disciple still living. Their pupils were each over one hundred years old, of course, but their presence helped to authenticate the teaching as it was transmitted. At this stage the *sutta*s and the Vinaya were written down in Sinhalese script using the Pali language. Today we can read Pali using the Roman alphabet.

At that time King Asoka, the great Buddhist king of India, had sent his son, the Venerable Mahindra, to Sri Lanka to propagate Buddhism. The king of Sri Lanka readily adopted this new teaching, and many noblemen became monks (*bhikkhus*). The monks undertook to put what we call the Pali canon into written form. In Pali this is called the *Tipiṭaka* (*ti* means three and *pitaka* means basket). There is a reason for this name. The original manuscript was written down on palm (*ola*) leaves with a *stilo*, a pointed steel dagger-like instrument, which scratched the letters into the soft leaves. An ink made from berries was rubbed over the whole page and then gently removed, so that only the indentations retained the color. Palm leaves were not bound like books but had to be carried around in baskets. Three separate ones were used: one for *sutta*s, one for Vinaya, and one for Abhidhamma, to keep them apart. Since that time, monks of Sri Lanka have copied the original palm leaves onto new ones in the same manner, because the leaves eventually crumble and fall apart. It is a matter of pride and tradition for the monks of the monastery built around the rock where Mahindra first preached the Dhamma to copy the original leaves year after year.

The written transmission has always been supported by oral transmission; reading a book can never be the same as hearing the Dhamma from a teacher. The oral transmission from the Buddha's time was passed from teacher to disciple in spite of political upheavals and natural disasters, and it continues to be so today.

In order to benefit from an oral transmission, one must listen with heart and mind. The mind conceptualizes; the heart believes without clearly understanding. Together they can grasp the meaning behind the words. Words are concepts, which can be twisted out of shape. Our minds are magicians and are capable of transforming one thing into another.

The teaching of the Buddha is like an enormous map showing a vast landscape with a roadway leading from here to there. It is his unique gift that this map is offered and made available to anyone who wants it. Naturally, not having traversed the whole length of the road, one cannot possibly know whether what lies ahead is correctly delineated. There is only one way of approaching that which one has not yet experienced, namely by opening heart and mind to hear whether truth is being expounded. The heart must summon up enough confidence to try the next step, otherwise conceptual thinking and logical conclusions will stand in the way.

This teaching, tried and true over the centuries, is one of the greatest jewels humanity possesses. The original words of the master are overpoweringly effective in changing pain and grief (*dukkha*) to happiness (*sukkha*). Access to it is through the heart and the mind. The Buddha recommended study and practice, so that knowledge can point the way and practice can do the work.

The discourse you will hear, called the *Upanisa Sutta* from the Connected Discourses (Saṃyutta Nikāya), teaches us the path from our present pain and grief to liberation. Can we do it in the scope of a seven-day meditation course? The Buddha says we can. In the *Satipaṭṭhāna Sutta*, the discourse on the foundations of mindfulness, the Buddha said that if one practices mindfulness for seven years one will definitely have the result either of becoming enlightened or not returning to the wheel of birth and death. Then he said, "Nay, not for seven years, even six years, five, four, three, two, or even one year. Even for eleven months, ten, nine, eight, seven, six, five, four, three, two, or even one month. Nay, even for seven days." That, of course, means mindfulness in its perfection. It is unusual, to say the least, to reach complete freedom in seven days, but it is certainly possible to explain the path of practice within that time.

There is a story about the Buddha taking a walk with his monks in the forest. Picking up a handful of leaves, he said to the monks, "Which are greater in number, the leaves on the trees or the leaves in my hand?" The monks said, "Sir, the leaves on the trees, of course, are far greater in number than those you have in your hand." The Buddha replied, "That's right. What I have taught you, compared with what I know, is like the leaves in my hand, but it is perfectly sufficient to attain liberation."

The authenticity of the *Tipiṭaka* can be felt when people who were present when the Buddha spoke are mentioned by name and profession. The place where the *sutta* was being taught is often described, and the same people occur so many times that one feels one actually knows them. Many of the *sutta*s start with the words "*Evam me suttam*," meaning "Thus have I heard," an opening used by the Venerable Ananda speaking at the first great council of enlightened ones. He went on to say where he heard the teaching and who else was present. This was to ensure that he was repeating the discourse correctly; in the case of discrepancies, those who had also been present could be asked to confirm his account.

We can feel enormous gratitude and joy to be among those people on earth who are able to hear the oral transmission of the Buddha's teaching.

Considering that there are more than five billion people on this planet, this is a most fortunate karma resultant. Joy and gratitude should be the two factors that open our hearts to the teaching. The mind alone does not suffice. Meditation generates certain experiences, always connected with feeling, which is our "heart quality."

The Buddha himself was a prince and lived in great luxury. He found that all the indulgences open to him and the luxury in which he lived did not bring him happiness. This certainly applies to today's society. We can have all the luxury and indulgences possible, and yet happiness escapes us. The Buddha felt that his luxurious life prevented his true understanding of reality. He left the palace and became an ascetic, mortifying his body for six years, but that too failed to bring the desired results. After having found his own way to enlightenment, he said that neither indulgence nor asceticism was right, but rather a middle path that avoided both extremes.

The middle path is always one of simplicity—of providing necessities, but nothing more. This simplicity can also be noticed in the teaching. There are few rituals, no initiations, and no secrets. The *sutta* that I have chosen for this meditation course contains all the elements needed for a complete spiritual path. As is common in the Buddha's expositions, it is a graduated path, which starts with our ordinary, everyday experience and gradually shows us how to gain access to liberation, to final freedom.

ᐳᕁ1 The "Why" and "How" of Meditation

THERE IS VERY LITTLE DOUBT that those of us who want to meditate are looking for something other than what we are used to in the world. We are already wise enough to know that the world hasn't fulfilled our expectations, and maybe we already know that it may never do so. That is a big step in itself.

When we sit down to meditate, we are trying to transcend our everyday consciousness, the consciousness used to transact ordinary business, the one used in the world's marketplace as we go shopping, bring up our children, work in an office or in our business, clean the house, check our bank statements, and all the rest of daily living. Everyone knows that kind of consciousness, and without it we can't function. It is our survival consciousness, and we need it for that. It cannot reach far enough or deep enough into the Buddha's teachings, because these are unique and profound; our everyday consciousness is neither unique nor profound, just utilitarian.

In order to attain the kind of consciousness that is capable of going deeply enough into the teachings to make them our own and thereby change our whole inner view, we need a mind with the ability to remove itself from the ordinary thinking process. Attaining this sort of mind is only possible through meditation. There is no other way. Meditation is therefore a means, and not an end in itself. It is a means to change the mind's capacity in such a way that it can perceive entirely different realities from the ones we are used to. The recognition that meditation is a tool is important, because it is often wrongly considered to be an end in itself. In Pali, meditation is called *bhāvanā*, "mind training," to be used for honing the mind until it becomes such a sharp tool that it cuts through everyday realities.

Most people sit down to meditate in order to make their minds peaceful. But a calm mind is only one of the two essential aspects of meditation. Insight (*vipassanā*) is the other. The goal of meditation is insight, and tranquility (*samatha*) is the means to that end. According to the Pali canon, the Buddha taught forty different methods of meditation, some used strictly for achieving calm and others for attaining insight. We do not need to practice that many.

Everybody is looking for some calm, some peace, and the ability to stop the mind from continuing its usual chatter. While it is necessary to cultivate the calm aspect of meditation, most people find it impossible to sit down and immediately become tranquil. Unfortunately, our minds are used to being exactly the opposite. They are thinking, evaluating, and judging from morning to night, and then dreaming from night to morning, so that they don't get a moment's rest. If we were to treat our bodies in that way we would soon be out of commission. The body can't handle that for more than a few days, never having a moment's rest, working all the time. When we ask this of our mind we are surprised that things don't turn out the way we hoped, and that the world doesn't work the way we thought it would. It would be even more surprising if it were otherwise, because what we see in our own mind is exactly what is going on in everybody else's. That, too, is an important aspect of the meditative mind—to realize that we are not individually burdened with all this unsatisfactoriness (*dukkha*). It is a universal aspect of existence, comprising the first noble truth of the Buddha's teaching.[1]

Unsatisfactoriness is universal. It doesn't belong to any one of us but to all of us. Because our minds are not yet trained, the world is the way it is, and meditation is a struggle. We need to learn to halt the habit patterns of the mind. Our minds are used to thinking, but when we want to become calm and peaceful, that is exactly what we have to stop doing. It is easier said than done, because the mind will continue to do what it is used to doing. There is another reason why the mind finds it difficult to refrain from its habits: thinking is the only ego support we have while we are meditating, and particularly when we keep noble silence. "I think, therefore I am"—some Western philosophy accepts that as an absolute. Actually, it is a relative truth that all of us experience.

When we are thinking, we know that we are here; when there is no chattering in the mind, we believe we have lost control. But actually, it's exactly the other way around. As long as we can't stop thinking, we have no control. We are in control of our mind only when we are able to stop thinking when we want to. The difficulty arising for most, if not all, meditators is this aspect of letting go. To let go of the only ego support we have while we are meditating, namely our thinking, has to be a deliberate act. When we go about our daily business we deliberately direct our mind toward what we want to do. If we want to work in the kitchen we deliberately go there and turn our attention to what needs to be done. If we have work to do in an office we deliberately turn our mind to letters, files, and other office business. It's the same in meditation.

Our first difficulty is that although we would like to become peaceful and calm and have no thoughts, our mind does not want to obey. It refuses to do so because then we would appear to have no support for our existence, and because our habits are against it. So instead of trying over and over again to become calm, we can use whatever arises to gain some insight. A little bit of insight brings a little bit of calm, and a little bit of calm brings a little bit of insight. Calm has no purpose other than to change our ordinary, everyday consciousness into a transcendental consciousness that is able to understand and use the teachings of the Buddha to change from an ordinary being into a transcendental being. If calm doesn't arise it is not a great problem, because whatever else does arise helps us to gain some insight into who we really are. This is the main reason for a meditation retreat. It is an inward journey to give us a little more understanding of who we are. Nothing could be more interesting, but there are some aspects from which we would like to run at times. We can't run away, while we are meditating, unless we start fantasizing and making up stories. Everybody is liable to do that, but when it does happen, let us realize that it is simply an escape.

To really further our inner journey, we are going to observe noble silence. Noble silence means not to talk to one another, which may be difficult when we are among friends. Take the difficulty as a challenge, and remember that challenges are steppingstones. Noble silence is one of the most effective tools for an inner journey. Usually we only have the opportunity for noble silence when we go on a retreat. Normally there are people around us with whom we communicate, which is one means of escape from our own suffering. Pain and grief is familiar to everyone even if we use different words for it, such as anger, fear, worry, upset, restlessness, and many others.

It is important to keep in mind that the very first noble truth the Buddha expounded upon enlightenment was that "unsatisfactoriness is." Unsatisfactoriness is a feature of existence. If we experience it in ourselves, we prove that the Buddha's teaching is correct. That's all. We don't need to start suffering over it, we can just observe it and say, "Evidence." There are innumerable things that expose us to unsatisfactoriness, but we can remember the first noble truth that "unsatisfactoriness is" and say, "That's right, that's what the Buddha taught."

The Buddha also propounded the second noble truth, namely that the reason for unsatisfactoriness is craving. We may look into ourselves and inquire, "What do I want that I am not getting? What am I getting that I don't want?" These are the two reasons, which are actually one and the same, for having unsatisfactoriness. There's only one way of dealing with suffering when it arises, and that's to drop the wanting; suffering will then disappear. Such insight is only possible when we stop going outward, through communication and through our many activities. We must have quiet times when we can really look inside ourselves.

Perhaps you have meditated before. Nevertheless, I will explain to you various meditation methods and their possible results. Whatever method we use is only valid if it brings results. If a certain method doesn't work, it's best to change it. There is nothing to hang on to where a meditation method is concerned. People have different tendencies and different characters, and although our minds may have the same potential and capacities, we do need different approaches. Some minds are visual and like pictures; some like words, telling stories; and some prefer numbers, putting everything in neat little boxes. There are minds that delight in attention to detail. We may already know what kind of mind we have, or we can experiment in meditation and see which one of the different methods is most conducive to our becoming calm.

Meditating on the breath is how one practices the first foundation of mindfulness, mindfulness of the body (*kāyānupassanā*). Such mindfulness should also extend to everything we do outside the meditation room, which is something we will often forget, but at least we should direct our attention toward that goal. It is pleasant to sit and try to become calm by watching the breath, but if we do not reinforce our practice with mindfulness outside the meditation sessions, it will not have the desired results. We cannot split our mind in two, one part for meditation and one for other activities. We have one mind and we have to train it as a whole, which extends to whatever we do: getting up, walking, opening or closing the door, any kind of work, always being fully attentive to the bodily action. Mindfulness of the body extends to having a shower, going to the toilet, getting up in the morning, taking off and putting on clothes. One of the bodily actions most conducive to mindfulness of the body is eating, because the eating process involves many physical actions.

No one can really teach us to be mindful. We teach ourselves, using landmarks and signposts. In our tradition we don't have gurus. We have people who reiterate the Buddha's words from the Pali canon and who may be able to give us some advice. Mindfulness can only be practiced and taught to oneself by oneself. Nobody can help us to be mindful; only we know when we are.

Being mindful means that mind and body are in the same place. "Washing dishes while washing dishes" is a famous phrase of Thich Nhat Hanh, a Vietnamese meditation teacher. Not thinking "I wish I had finished," or "Why are they using so many dishes?" or "I'm glad I don't have to do this tomorrow," or "Why do I always end up washing dishes?"—nothing like that. Just washing dishes, that's all. The same applies to eating: not "I like this. I wonder how they made it?" Just eating. This applies to all other physical actions. The Buddha said, "The one way for the purification of beings, for the elimination of pain, grief, and lamentation, for the final ending of all pain and grief, for entering the noble path, for attaining liberation, is mindfulness." What more do we want? We all have some mindfulness; we just have to cultivate it.

Meditation is the means by which we can practice mindfulness to the point where insight becomes so strong that we can see absolute reality behind the relative. Mindfulness trained in meditation can then continue in every activity. Here we are only considering mindfulness of body action, because we make use of the body constantly. As the body can be touched and seen, we have a chance of really having mind and body in the same place, instead of letting the mind run off into its usual ramifications while the body does something else. If we were to keep mind and body in one place we would have no problem watching the breath, because that is all that is really happening—we are breathing. Nothing else. Everything else is conjecture.

When we keep our attention on the breath, the mind, being with the breath, is actually mindful. This is called "mindfulness of in-breath/out-breath" or *ānâpanāsati* in Pali. We will notice again and again that the mind just does not wish to stay attentive but wants to stray to something else. We will use this straying to gain insight into ourselves. We won't just say, "Thinking, thinking," because that doesn't tell us anything new; rather, we shall learn to label. We are going to say "past," "future," or "nonsense" (the last nearly always fits). We can say "wanting," "hoping," or "planning." The last one is very popular. We think we can't get anything done while we are sitting, so at least we can plan what to do next week. The first label that comes to mind should be used; we need not try to find exactly the right label, because that induces new thinking.

If thoughts are like clouds in the background, not solid but quick to disappear, it is unnecessary to run after them with a label. But if thoughts are solid, it is helpful to label them. Labeling then has two results. First of all, it dissolves the thought, because the mind can't do two things simultaneously. Giving a label means watching the thought objectively and not becoming involved in it. Therefore, it dissolves like a water bubble. The second very useful result of labeling is some insight into our own thinking process and patterns. This insight is extremely important, because it helps the meditator not to fall into the error of always believing his or her own thinking. Only people who never meditate believe what they are thinking. When one has labeled one's thoughts in meditation, one realizes that the thinking process is quite arbitrary and often has no real meaning—it is nonsense, there is no sense in it, and it is not even wanted.

Gaining such an insight into our thinking during meditation helps us in everyday life to drop thoughts that are not useful, and this makes our life less stressful. If we can drop a thought by labeling it during meditation we can do the same in daily life. Otherwise we have meditated in vain—we have been sitting and getting sore knees without any result. We must be able to transfer our meditation practice into everyday life.

In meditation we drop all thoughts. When they recur, we drop them again. Instead of thinking, we put our attention on the breath. In daily life we drop unwholesome thoughts and substitute wholesome ones. It's exactly the same substitution process, and when we have learned it in meditation it can become a good habit in daily life. Not that it will always work (there's no such thing as always), but we understand the possibilities.

When we listen to the words of the Buddha, we know that he is showing us an ideal to work for, and that if we have not yet reached that ideal, we need not blame ourselves. "Awareness, no blame, change" is an important formula to remember: become aware of what is going on within, but do not attach any blame to it. Things are the way they are, but we, as thinking human beings, have the ability to change, and that is what we are doing in meditation. We can drop the thought and go back to noticing our breath, and the more often we do this, the easier and more natural it becomes. Eventually the mind gives in and says, "All right then, I'll stop all this thinking for a while." Not only does this become easier because it has become a habit, but we shall be more and more determined to abandon discursive, nondirectional thinking, because it will have become apparent how unnecessary it really is. It brings no results, it goes around in circles, and it is disturbing. Thus, the mind recognizes the value of staying with the subject of meditation.

If we can learn to use mindfulness of the breath in meditation, then we have a very good grip on mindfulness in everyday life. One supports the other. It is impossible to make two people out of each one of us; we are training only one mind. Obviously, the time spent on our daily activities far exceeds the time we spend in meditation. Therefore, we cannot just drop all training when we step out of the meditation room.

There are five ways of using the breath. The most traditional is also the most difficult, but it is the most productive of calm. We simply notice the breath at the nostrils as it moves in and out. In our tradition we watch both in- and out-breaths; we do not wish to give the mind a chance to wander off into its usual discursiveness, but want it to stay with the breath at all times. The wind of the breath creates a sensation when it touches the nostrils, which helps one to focus at that point. This is the most "one-pointed" way of concentrating on the breath and is particularly useful for experienced meditators. "One-pointed" means being in one spot only, which is a very important aspect of meditation. Because the attention is focused on one point only, it helps the mind to become sharp and unwavering.

We can use various support systems to help us remain mindful of the breath. One of these is counting the breaths. We count "one" on the in-breath, "one" on the out-breath, "two" on the in-breath, "two" on the out-breath, all the way up to ten. Every time the mind wanders off we return to "one," no matter whether we were at four, five, or eight. This is a good method for people who like numbers and who have orderly, organized minds.

Some people are not very fond of numbers but prefer words. Try using the word "peace" on the in-breath, "peace" on the out-breath. Actually, any word will do. We could use "peace" on the in-breath and "love" on the out-breath, filling ourselves with peace and extending love outward. However, it is preferable to use just one word, because the more input there is into the mind, the less calm it becomes. It is sufficient to keep the attention focused on "peace" on the in-breath, filling ourselves with it, and "peace" on the out-breath, letting it flow outward. This is very useful to those to whom words are important.

If we don't like either numbers or words, then we can use a picture—for example, we can experience the breath as if it were a cloud that fills us when we breathe in. The out-breath can be visualized as a cloud coming out to envelop us. Some people see the cloud as taking on different shapes: larger on the out-breath and smaller when it is taken in through the nostrils. Any support for concentration is better than discursive thinking; using visualization is not as one-pointed as just watching the breath, but it's much better than thinking about what happened last week, or what might happen next week.

There is another method that is helpful to those who are still new to meditation. We follow the in-breath into the body and notice it wherever it becomes apparent. It goes in through the nostrils and up the nose; we can feel it in the throat and in the lungs, as far down as the stomach; then we can follow it leaving the body again. We do not search for the sensations created by the breath, but we put our attention on all the spots, where they become apparent to us, both when breathing in and when breathing out. This is a particularly useful method for meditators who are primarily concerned with feelings. The inner feelings connected with the inhaling and exhaling of the breath become apparent and can keep the mind attentive and centered on one's inner being. This greatly helps to reduce the mind's tendency to connect to outer happenings through thinking and reacting.

The last method of attending to sensations connected with the breath is to be aware of filling oneself with breath and emptying oneself out again. That, too, is useful as a means for concentration.

We have considered five different methods of using in-breaths and out-breaths. Use only one method at a time. Pick the one that feels comfortable and use it during one meditation session. If it seems impossible to concentrate even slightly, try another method at the next meditation session. Do not change methods during one sitting.

If the mind wants to run off, it is useful to direct the attention toward the impermanence of the breath. The untrained mind always wants to think, but at least we can give it something useful to think about. It doesn't have to be allowed to think about whatever it pleases, but rather it can think about how each in-breath finishes, then each out-breath likewise—constant change, on which our life depends. We could not stay alive without our breath coming and going all the time. If we were to keep the in-breath, we would be dead within a few minutes; the same would occur if we were to hang on to the out-breath. This is an important insight that can link the mind to the impermanent aspect of each person, particularly ourselves.

If the mind already has a certain ability to stay with the breath, let it remain there, but if there is a constant thought process, one thought after another, direct the mind toward impermanence. Attention to that aspect of the breath gives rise to a question: if life depends on such an in- and out-flow, what can we find within us that doesn't come and go? Then the mind may turn within and may be able to stay on the breath a little more easily.

Everybody likes to have some calm and peace, and should have them, too, otherwise meditation becomes a chore and never a pleasant abiding. But we do need directives for insight, especially as Westerners. We have been trained from kindergarten on to investigate, to find out, and to ponder. Naturally, we are still doing that, and it is difficult for our minds to stop on demand. So we have to allow for all possible approaches in our meditation.

Experiencing the impermanence of the breath brings useful insight and is immensely preferable to thoughts about the past or the future. Being able to stay with the breath means that we are mindfully "in the moment." Absurd as it may seem, without training we hardly ever manage to do this. We can only live life each moment, and yet we are concerned with the past, which has gone irrevocably, and with the future, which is nothing but a hope and a prayer. When the future really comes, it is always called the present. We can never experience the future; it is nothing but a concept. If we want to gain wisdom, we have to experience life, and the only way we will ever do so is to be in each moment. The more we train the mind to be in each moment, the more we will actually know what human life means. Otherwise we will be either remembering or planning. This is where labeling helps us. To be present now means to be with each breath. We cannot watch a breath that is past, nor one that is still in the future. We can only watch the one that is happening. This is a very useful way of understanding how our minds work. The Buddha didn't want us to believe his statements without question but to have enough confidence to investigate them. They are in fact nothing but directions, guidelines, and signposts, to try out for ourselves.

What we consider a good posture for meditation is a straight but relaxed back, which means relaxing the shoulders by lifting them and letting them fall, relaxing the stomach, which is also a point of tension, and relaxing the neck. Keep the legs in a position where they will feel comfortable for some time. Hands can be on the knees, palms up or palms down, or together in the lap. We meditate with our eyes closed. If we feel drowsy, we open them immediately, look at any light, move the body to increase blood circulation, and then close them again.

Any painful feelings that arise can be used as a means to gain insight. Painful feelings are useful to teach us two important lessons. When we get a painful feeling, in this case physical, our immediate reaction is "I want to get rid of it." This is how we live our lives and this is how we remain in the round of rebirth (*saṃsāra*). We want to eliminate pain and yet keep the pleasant feelings, but that can't be done. Nobody can win that battle, so the sooner we find out that this is not a skillful way of dealing with pain, the easier it becomes for us to deal with unpleasant feelings in daily living.

The pain that arises during meditation does so in a certain way, which is important to recognize. There is touch contact of the knee on the pillow, or there may be the contact of the left foot on the thigh—wherever the pain is, there is touch contact. All our sense contacts generate feelings. The enlightened one also has feelings, of which there are only three kinds: pleasant, unpleasant, and neutral. We usually consider the neutral ones as quite pleasant because at least they are not unpleasant, so we actually only deal with pleasant and unpleasant feelings. We are concerned with them during most of our waking hours. From touch contact arises feeling, and from that comes perception, the realization that "this is painful" or "this is not nice." Let's say that we call it "pain." Then comes the immediate, impulsive reaction in the mind (which is also karma-making): "I don't like it," "I want to get rid of it," "I've got to move," "This could be dangerous, my blood circulation is stopping," and other thoughts like that.

The mental formations (*sankhāra*) are also our karma formations. We make karma first by thought, then by speech, and lastly by action. At the moment of thought we have already made slightly negative karma through negativity in the mind. This is not a great problem because it arises out of an impulsive, instinctive human tendency, but if we want to transcend our human problems and our marketplace consciousness, we also have to transcend our instinctive reactions. We could think, "This is an unpleasant feeling called pain, but I didn't ask for it, so why am I calling it mine? Isn't it just something that happened?"

Here we learn detachment, to let go of the unpleasantness and get back to the subject of meditation. Everybody can do that for a limited time. How limited that time is, is an individual matter. When the unpleasant feeling calls us again, we can repeat the same thought process. We may also recognize that the body always has some pain, and that we only suffer because we are not accepting that fact. Without the resistance to pain and the craving to change it, there would be no stress. There may come a moment when the mind says, "This is all very well, but I can't handle any more of this pain." Then we change our position gently, slowly, so as not to disturb our neighbor, or our own mind, or admit to ourselves that we have been conquered by our own unpleasant feelings.

That's perfectly all right. We are often conquered by our feelings, but here we have a chance to realize it. We are conquered because we suffer, owing to our unpleasant feelings. If we could allow an unpleasant feeling simply to be an unpleasant feeling, which it really is, and not react to it, we would have conquered ourselves. This is therefore a very important inner journey. It is useless to sit there with teeth clenched and say, "I'm going to sit through this if it's the last thing I do," or "I am going to show them that I can do it." This attitude is connected with hate and not with insight. We have all experienced pain in our lives; now we can gain insight by noticing our reactions to it. This is a very helpful way of using unpleasantness in the body.

Another way to use unpleasantness is to keep the mind focused on the painful feeling, making it one's subject of meditation. This is only possible if one does not dislike the feeling; otherwise there is only rejection in the mind. Unwavering attention on the unpleasant feeling provides an opportunity to recognize its changeable nature. The feeling may then actually dissolve completely.

To sum up, we can either get back to mindfulness of breathing by detaching ourselves from the feeling, or by using it for our subject of meditation. We may also be conquered by it at times.

If the weather permits, we can walk outside. Walking meditation has several advantages. First of all, it gives the body a chance to move after sitting still for some time. It also leads us into mindfulness in an activity that we use in daily living. We do a lot of walking in our lives, so if we learn to be attentive and mindful in walking meditation, it is quite easy to transfer that to our daily life.

The essential aspect of walking meditation is exactly the same as the attention on the in-breath and out-breath. It is designed to keep the mind focused on a physical movement. Whereas in the first case we were watching the movement of the breath, in walking meditation we are watching the movement of the feet. The same opportunities for calm and insight exist in both methods.

Choose your own walking path, approximately twenty-five paces long. Mark the beginning and the end of the path by selecting a rock or a bush or whatever may be there. Do not intersect with another person, because that is disturbing to both. Either walk parallel or find a space that isn't being used by someone else. We should look down, because if we look around we can be distracted by the scenery and pay attention to the trees, flowers, and birds rather than to walking. We keep our eyes open, and they automatically look down in front of our feet. Hands can be held together either in front of us or behind us, so that they don't move and distract us. The attention can be on a threefold or a sixfold movement of the feet. Threefold means raising the foot, carrying it, and putting it down. The second foot is raised only when the first is completely down, which slows walking automatically and also prevents us from having two simultaneous movements. Usually we just touch the ground and immediately raise the other foot. The pace at which we walk is up to each individual—whatever is suitable. In the threefold movement we can just watch the action, or we can count "one, two, three" in the mind while watching the movement. We can say, "Raising, carrying, putting down," in order to help us pay attention.

It is very helpful to stand still for a moment if the mind goes off into discursive thinking. Again, labeling will help. If it is massive thinking, standing still already helps to let go of that. It doesn't matter how often we stand still; there are no value judgments. There's nothing but awareness, no judging of oneself or others. It is simply knowing what is going on within. Mindfulness is knowing only, so if we know what's going on, we can label the thought, as we did when we were sitting, or stand still to encourage bare attention once more.

We can also use the sixfold movement. We take the foot off the ground, lifting first the heel, then the rest of the foot, followed by raising, carrying, putting down the heel, then the rest of the foot. Being more complicated, this requires more mindfulness, and those who like numbers can count from one to six as an aid. When there is greater concentration, we can dispense with counting. Those who like words could say, "Heel, sole, raising, carrying, heel, sole," as an aid to concentration. Those who tend to visualization can imagine that when raising the foot there is a flower embedded in the ground underneath which now has a chance to grow. As the foot is carried forward the flower opens up, and as the foot is put down the flower closes again.

We can also realize that the earth does not object when we stamp on it, walk on it, or spit on it and will always patiently endure, which is a quality we can develop within ourselves. Whatever we do—putting the foot down hard or gently—the earth will not object. When we walk on grass, we could notice that the grass bends under our foot, but as we raise our foot again the grass stands up straight. This is a quality that the Buddha compared to being like bamboo—bending in the storm of pain and grief, but never breaking. The grass also exemplifies this ability of acceptance.

All these are "mind crutches" to help us stay with the subject rather than thinking of extraneous matters. Sensations are another aid to staying focused on the movement. When the foot is down on the ground, there is a solid feeling, a touch sensation. As we raise it, the sensation becomes an airy feeling. As we push forward, there's a feeling of movement breaking through the resistance of inertia, and as we put the foot down again, we have a solid touch once more. These feelings are very helpful in keeping our attention on the action, as otherwise it can become quite automatic, with only half-focused attention. This is not mindfulness. For the three-fold movement, we can use the same "mind crutches."

Just as we can realize and observe that the breath is in constant flux and only keeps us alive when it is so, in the same way the movement of the feet is an ever-recurring, changing flow. We can use our body only when that quality of infinite change is present, graphically illustrating one of the three characteristics of all existence: impermanence. This observation leads to insight, while uninterrupted attention on the subject of meditation leads to calm. Both have to be practiced in conjunction with each other.

QUESTIONS

STUDENT: *As part of noble silence, should one avoid eye contact, since that is communication also?*

AYYA KHEMA: It is very useful to avoid eye contact. Nobody should think that the other person is unfriendly or doesn't like one, but should realize that he or she is protecting his or her inner journey.

S: *Are the five methods of using the breath practiced in addition to the basic method of following the breath, or do we substitute them for that?*

AK: The first method is the traditional way of watching, or following, the breath. The next four are support systems to give the mind a little more to do besides watching the breath. We can choose one of the five methods depending upon our own inclinations.

S: *Are you still watching the breath when you use the other four support systems?*

AK: Yes. You watch the breath and count it, or watch the breath and name it, or watch the breath and picture it, or watch the breath and notice feelings. The breath is always the main subject; the others are supports.

S: *In all five methods, with the exception of counting, isn't the process of labeling whatever arises a form of discursiveness?*

AK: No. Labeling helps us to gain insight into our habitual thought process, no matter which of the methods of watching the breath we employ, including counting.

S: *I recall in your instructions you said to go back to "one" if you lose track while counting the breath.*

AK: If the thought that arises is to be clearly known, it is a good practice to label it and then to go back to "one," if the method of counting the breath is being used.

S: *And you use the first label that comes to your mind?*

AK: The first label that comes to mind is usually correct anyway. If we don't use the first thought, we may have discursive thoughts about the label.

S: *So if one just says, "Oh, that's—"?*

AK: No, that's not a label, that's an exclamation. A label is something that identifies, like food packages in a supermarket, for example. If we go through a supermarket and take many tins and cartons without looking at the labels, we might end up with a lot of cat food, and may not even have a cat at home. The label on the tin tells us what is inside. If the tins were just labeled "oh," we might collect a lot of cat food without knowing what we were doing. The identification labels can be "future," "past," "nonsense," "hoping," "planning," "remembering," "wanting," "identifying," or any others that may come to mind.

⚛ 2 The Heart Essence

OUR EMOTIONS ARE a very significant part of our makeup, and it's in our emotions that we often encounter difficulties. The Buddha spoke about four supreme emotions, which are the only ones worth having. All others can be usefully discarded, or replaced with one of the four. They are called in Pali the *brahmavihāra*, the *brahma*s being gods, and a *vihāra* being an abode, a place to live in. Therefore, these emotions are the "divine abodes." In one respect, they are the vehicles for the god realms, those realms that are nonphysical, and in another they are the emotions that enable us as human beings to live here and now in a more refined atmosphere of our own consciousness.

Purification of emotions brings clarification of thought. We all know what it is like when we are in the grip of strong emotions—they are like ocean waves, pulling us down until we can't see anything but water. In the same way, we are unable to see clearly while we are at the mercy of our emotions. The clarification of our thinking process has at its root the purification of the emotions, so that we are no longer under the influence or in the grip of these strong passions that make it impossible to see clearly.

The whole of the spiritual path is one of purification, which means a constant letting go. It is a matter of seeing our inner difficulties and learning to drop them. Meditation is our vehicle for practicing the art of letting go.

The four supreme emotions are loving-kindness (*mettā*), compassion (*karunā*), sympathetic joy (*muditā*), and equanimity (*upekkhā*). I want to talk specifically about loving-kindness. These words are more meaningful than they may seem. In Pali the word *mettā* is powerful, and so is the Sanskrit equivalent *maitri*. For us, "loving-kindness" is rather dull; it doesn't really tell us much. The word "love" is not commonly used as a translation for *mettā*, because we have the wrong concept of love. But if we were to use the word "love" it would have much more of an impact upon us, because it means something very definite. We have all experienced it to some degree, yet it does not convey the same emotion as loving-kindness.

When we think of love, we think of an emotion that is directed toward one specific person, or perhaps two, three, or four people one happens to be very fond of. We also can think of love as something that we direct toward a certain ideal, such as love of one's country, or love of a certain activity. We give direction to our love and also imbue it with one very important condition, namely that it should be reciprocated. When there is love in our heart for someone, we think it is a tragedy if that other person doesn't return our love. None of this has anything to do with loving-kindness; it does not even come near to describing loving-kindness. The kind of love that we are used to and that we deal with in our daily lives does not have the purity of loving-kindness. If we direct our love toward one person and expect to be loved, then our love is tinged with fear—we are afraid to lose that person's love. We can never equate fear with love; fear is always due to hate. We don't hate that person, but we hate the possibility of losing the person, or the person's love, or the comforts of our situation as it is. We are only familiar with a love that has built-in fear. Naturally, this is not satisfying, and in the normal run of things we believe this to be the fault of the other person; therefore, we feel we must go out and find someone else. We might even think it is our own fault, but none of this helps us to find fulfillment or satisfaction. The divine or supreme emotions, however, can give us completeness, because they do not have any negativity in them.

Loving-kindness is a quality of our own heart. It has nothing to do with being loved back, or with one or more specific persons, or with any ideal or activity or any particular direction. It is simply the training of our heart. Just as meditation is training of the mind and does not depend on any input into the mind, the same goes for loving-kindness in the heart.

In Pali, heart and mind are one word, *citta*, but in English, we have to differentiate between the two to make the meaning clear. When we attend to the mind, we are concerned with the thinking process, with the intellectual understanding that derives from knowledge, and with our ability to retain knowledge and make use of it. When we speak of "heart" we think of feelings and emotions, our ability to respond with our fundamental being. Although we may believe that we are leading our lives according to our thinking process, that is not the case. If we examine this question more closely, we will find that we are leading our lives according to our feelings, and that our thinking is dependent upon our feelings. The emotional aspect of ourselves is of such great importance that its purification is the basis for a harmonious and peaceful life, and also for good meditation.

When we talk about loving-kindness in the Buddha's way, we are thinking of a warm and kind feeling toward others. It is not a matter of judging others—whether they are worthy of love, or willing to love us back, or become our friends and supporters, or even whether they want our love. It is strictly a matter of clearing out our negative reactions, which are often based on negative facts. Dislike is never justified. Only our discrimination between right and wrong is appropriate. We can find unwholesomeness in ourselves and in others, but that does not allow us to use our emotions in a negative way. We can compare this to a mother with her child. Perhaps the mother has just cleaned her house when her small child comes in and thoughtlessly makes it dirty again. This will not be a reason for the mother to stop loving the child, but she will most likely tell the child that this was not a good thing to do. We do not lose our ability to discriminate between good and bad, but when we purify our hearts we abandon our negative reactions.

We can start with ourselves. If we can see our own mistakes, and neither dislike them nor hate ourselves for them but simply see them and accept them, we may then resolve to change. We will also learn to accept the fact that the determination to change and the actual change will not coincide. The actual change takes time. By accepting the difficulties in ourselves and seeing them clearly, we have the beginning of an understanding of others. Other people have similar difficulties—often identical ones. This is one of the great advantages, and a unique factor in the Buddha's teachings: he showed us that we are all made of the same ingredients; we all have the same pain and grief and we are all yearning for relief.

If we can see first of all what is happening within us and learn to accept and love ourselves in spite of all these difficulties, we have a good start. If we don't begin with ourselves, we have no way of actually, truly loving others. Very often people say (and mean it quite sincerely) that they find it difficult to love themselves but they are happy to love others. It's a myth. They love others of whom they approve, but not unconditionally. We have first to love ourselves unconditionally before we have the same open heart for all beings. Loving-kindness is just that: unconditional love. We do not lose our discrimination, for this would mean losing some of our intelligence, which would be a great disaster. What we lose is our judgmental attitude toward ourselves and others.

We are trying to accept things as they are, and will eventually succeed, consequently losing much of our suffering. Suffering is the constant push and pull against that which is. When we resist and push against something, for instance a door that won't open, our hand starts to hurt after a while; but if we accept the fact that the door won't open and go around another way, then there is no pain. Our suffering comes from our resistance, from wanting people and situations to be different. We don't like them the way they are and, moreover, we don't even want to live according to the laws of nature. Yet we really have no choice, which causes us a lot of grief.

It is the same with loving-kindness. We try to love that which we consider lovable. Someone else might not have the same opinion about what is lovable because his or her viewpoint is different. In the discourse "The All Embracing Net of Views," the Buddha described, under sixty-two headings, all the viewpoints we could ever have, and he said that they were all wrong because they were based on our ego concept. "I think," "I have that opinion," "I view it this way"—all distorted by our self-delusion and therefore never right in the absolute sense. If we can remember that we can never be absolutely correct, only right in a relative sense, then it may help us to drop our judgmental attitudes. We must begin with ourselves. Then we can relax and feel at ease, and once we can relax within ourselves we have a chance to meditate properly.

The Buddha said that in order to meditate properly one has to be comfortable in mind and body. We need a benevolent feeling toward ourselves, not only to give us ease in our daily lives, but also to succeed in our meditation. To relax within doesn't mean that we no longer know what our defilements are but that we realize that they, too, are acceptable. We can think of the process as akin to a child growing up. We do not expect a four-year-old to pass university examinations. We do not even expect him to pass a fifth-year test. He will grow up gently, slowly, in his own time. The Buddha likened us to children who are playing in a house that is on fire, who refuse to let go of their toys so that they can run out of the house and save themselves. The house on fire is the round of rebirth, and we won't let go of our toys, our computers, our cars, our houses, and particularly our bodies and minds, which we think belong to us. If we consider ourselves as children who need to grow up, who need time and gentle attention, then our mistakes are acceptable while the growing up process is taking place.

The acceptance of ourselves is the first step toward loving-kindness. It has to exist within us, for ourselves, because only then can we feel it, only then do we know what it is like. Loving-kindness's obvious enemy is hate, but its subtle enemy is affection. For most people that sounds peculiar, because affection is supposed to be a good thing. But affection is the enemy of loving-kindness, because it is based on attachment. If we are attached to one, two, three, or even ten people, then we can't reach outward; we are stuck. Attachment creates partiality, holding us back from transcending our judgmental attitudes. The love we need to have for ourselves is concerned with our wellbeing and growth, but it does not include our ego-centered bias. To distinguish between the two is difficult and can only be done by constant introspection. Loving oneself makes it easy to be with oneself, pleasant to be alone without being lonely. It does not include needing to have more, be more, and become more, all of which represent our search for more ego support. Pure loving-kindness is obstructed by our attachment to others and ourselves. When we are filled with feelings toward specific people and with a desire to be something special, great, clever, beautiful, or whatever it is we have in mind, there isn't enough space left to feel warmth toward all beings.

Loving-kindness is greatly helped by meditative insights that show us that our separation from one another is an illusion. When we discover that all of us are parts of the same whole, and when we actually feel that in meditation, it becomes so much easier to have the same love for ourselves and for others. It is not a passionate emotion but a harmonious, friendly, accepting, and peaceful feeling for oneself and other people. The Buddha's path leads away from passion toward dispassion.

Loving-kindness is to be extended toward all beings and all manifestations, yet most of our difficulties lie with people. It is much easier to love birds, dogs, cats, and trees than it is to love people. Trees and animals don't answer back, but people do, so this is where our training commences. We should consider practicing loving-kindness as part of our spiritual growth project. You will find guided loving-kindness meditations throughout this book; they are a means of directing the mind toward this aspect of our emotional purification.

Sometimes people find they don't feel anything while practicing loving-kindness meditation. That is nothing to worry about; thoughts aimed often enough in the right direction eventually produce the right feelings. All our sense contacts produce feelings. Thoughts are the sixth sense, and even if we are only thinking loving-kindness, eventually the feeling will arise. Thinking is one means of helping us to gain this heart quality, but certainly not the only one.

In our daily activities all of us are confronted with other people and often with those whom we would rather avoid. These are our challenges, lessons, and tests. If we consider them in that manner, we won't be so irritated by these experiences, nor will we be so apt to think, "I wish this wasn't happening," or "I wish he'd go away," or "I wish he would never say another word," thereby creating pain and grief for ourselves. When we realize that such a confrontation is exactly what we need at that moment in order to overcome resistance and negativity and to substitute loving-kindness for those emotions, then we will be grateful for the opportunity. Eventually we will find (mostly in retrospect, of course) that we can be very grateful to those people who have made life most difficult for us.

In overcoming that hurdle we took a big step ahead. If we keep on remembering the wrongs we have suffered, then our growth is retarded. Overcoming resistance, aversion, and negative reactions is the path of purification, the spiritual path, which can happen nowhere else except in our own heart and mind. It can never happen outside of us and only works with mindfulness and introspection. When we see clearly, we can change.

We will not succeed each time when our heart and mind are negatively involved, but such occasions will certainly remind us of what we are actually trying to do. When we completely forget, we are not practicing at all. Half the spiritual life consists of remembering what we are up against and where we are going. Loving-kindness, unconditional love, is not an easy thing to develop, but it is essential.

When we are confronted with people whom we may not even dislike, we are often oblivious to them or neutral toward them; that's the time to cultivate our loving feelings. When we use words and deeds to show other people that we care we grow in purification. When we suddenly remember, "I need to educate my heart," then we can do so deliberately. That brings results. Because there are so many obstructions within, overcoming them again and again brings enormous benefits. As a secondary result, others have the benefit of our love, but our own purification is the primary gain.

The stronger our loving-kindness, the more its influence will spread around us as a natural emanation of our being. The Buddha's loving-kindness was so strong that he was able to tame a wild elephant. Such may not be our ability, but with one's own inner purity of loving-kindness our whole environment can become uplifted. A person full of loving-kindness doesn't feel other people's negativity so much. Others are nothing but mirrors that reflect only what is in front of them—namely, ourselves. Whatever we see in others is exactly what is embedded in ourselves, so we might as well use that mirror image for our learning process. A person who has access to loving-kindness within his heart will not see much in others that is difficult to bear. Our life becomes smooth and harmonious, as does our spiritual practice.

We all know the sense of wellbeing that is generated when we feel positive and loving toward other people. We also know how unpleasant it feels for us when we are negative and full of dislike for others. If we have any sense at all, we want to make our own life easier, more pleasant, smoother, and more harmonious. We can observe that when we change our own feelings and emotions, things around us alter too. The extent of the changes around us depends on the strength of our loving-kindness. We may not be able to reach beings far and wide, but certainly the atmosphere in our vicinity will change for the better.

A person with a great deal of loving-kindness acts like a magnet. People are always drawn to that. However, if one wants to experience loving-kindness, one has to have it oneself. There is no other way, because another person's loving-kindness, while pleasant, immediately disappears when that person goes away. We can't hang on to another person, no matter who they are; it would create dependency on someone else, while the path we have chosen teaches independence. Moreover another's loving-kindness demonstrates their purification and does not encourage our own growth. We have to generate the feeling of loving-kindness within ourselves. Everyone can do it, though some people find it easier than others. It is a matter of working at it.

All of us suffer from ego delusion, which brings hate and greed in its wake. Those people who have more greed find loving-kindness easier than those who have more hate. The latter have other advantages, though. They are more likely to stick to the practice because they feel so much more uncomfortable. A great meditation master in Thailand once said that he would prefer that all his monks had more hate than greed. People with hate are harder to live with, but they practice with enthusiasm because they are so keen to change. An important part of our spiritual growth, one for which no special occasion is needed, is to practice loving-kindness toward people at all times, whether while shopping, going to the post office, meeting somebody on the street, or answering the phone. There is always an opportunity to practice. So many opportunities facilitate our growth, but can also make it more difficult because we may often forget. Hearing and remembering are two main aspects of the teaching. Only when we remember can we eventually make the Dhamma our own. Otherwise we have nothing to work with.

Mettā is a beautiful word—just five letters signifying the purity of our own heart, the heart essence, often obscured, yet always available.

Questions

STUDENT: *It seems that we feel attachment to ourselves but not much real affection. For others, there's both affection and attachment, but for ourselves, it seems to be attachment only.*

AYYA KHEMA: Actually, we do feel both for ourselves, but it wavers—sometimes we feel more of one than of the other. We need to find a balance where we have true acceptance of ourselves and not just this great ego-centeredness that is attachment.

We won't be able to get rid of it entirely until we have lost at least some of our ego illusion. But we can work on it whenever we see that our great attachment to ourselves is detrimental because it causes suffering. When we have a feeling of ease with ourselves, when we can be pleasantly alone without needing constant outside support, we are succeeding in the balancing act within. We may be aware of the attachment to ourselves, but it contains affection, and we can see how they go together when we observe how we act toward ourselves. We don't want anything to happen to us, not even a scratch. When we don't like to see a scratch on someone else, we certainly consider that as affection, don't we?

3 Guided Contemplations and Loving-Kindness Meditations

THE SENTENCES THAT FOLLOW should be spoken aloud. I will elaborate a little on the subject of each to help with the contemplation. To start with, fix your attention on the breath for a few moments.

Now say the first sentence:

MAY I BE FREE FROM ENMITY.

We can investigate whether we have had, or have now, any enmity, thoughts of resistance, rejection, aversion, feelings of not being friendly toward any living being. If there is any such feeling present now or remembered, then we contemplate how to change that into loving-kindness.

MAY I BE FREE FROM HURTFULNESS.

We reflect on whether we have hurt any living being in the past, or have had the intention of doing so. If we have, how can we change that in order that it will not occur again?

MAY I BE FREE FROM TROUBLES OF MIND AND BODY.

We contemplate whether there are any problems in mind or body and try to find their underlying cause. Then we practice letting go of the disturbance through nonclinging.

MAY I BE ABLE TO PROTECT MY OWN HAPPINESS.

We have to investigate what we consider to be our own happiness. When we are sure what it consists of, how can we go about protecting it from being disturbed or shattered?

WHATEVER BEINGS THERE ARE, MAY THEY BE FREE
FROM ENMITY.

We wish the same benefits for others that we have contemplated for ourselves. First, we need to know how to go about it ourselves. Then we may be able to help others to act likewise, and our own peacefulness will spread outward.

WHATEVER BEINGS THERE ARE, MAY THEY BE FREE
FROM HURTFULNESS.

We would like to have others share in what we ourselves have already experienced. If we are harmless, we can generate that feeling in others. Our contemplation consists in finding out how hurtfulness in mind, speech, and action can be eliminated.

WHATEVER BEINGS THERE ARE, MAY THEY BE FREE
FROM TROUBLES OF MIND AND BODY.

Here we can find out how much compassion we have for others. Do we really empathize with them?

WHATEVER BEINGS THERE ARE, MAY THEY BE ABLE
TO PROTECT THEIR OWN HAPPINESS.

If we have true lovingness and compassion for others, we will never disturb their happiness. We will be careful, and help them to protect it. We need to investigate how much of that we really feel and how to enlarge upon it.

GUIDED LOVING-KINDNESS MEDITATION I

First, concentrate on the breath for just a moment.

Let compassion arise in your heart for yourself and for all the pain and grief that has already happened in this life, is there now, and may yet come. Feel compassion for the lack of realization and compassion for the difficulties of the practice. Let this feeling embrace you and hold you safe and secure.

Extend the compassion from your heart to the person sitting nearest you. Extend compassion for all the pain and grief in his or her life that has been, is now, and may yet come, and compassion for the difficulties arising in meditation. Embracing the person, holding him or her tightly, give him or her a sense of being cared for.

Extend your compassion to everyone meditating with you, remembering that everyone has pain and grief. Remembering that everyone would like care and concern, embrace everyone with your compassion.

Think of your parents. Let the compassion for their difficulties and their pain and grief arise in your heart. Embrace them, showing them your care and concern.

Think of those people nearest and dearest to you. Have compassion for their pain and grief, their difficulties, their pain. Embrace them with your love and compassion, showing your care and concern.

Thinking of all your friends, let compassion arise in your heart. Let them know that you care, that you empathize with them. Embrace them with that feeling.

Think of anyone whom you find difficult to love, and think of that person with a feeling of compassion arising in you. Feel compassion for that person's pain, grief, and difficulties, for his or her lack of both freedom and liberation. Let this compassion really reach out to that person, filling and surrounding him or her with it.

Think of all those people whose lives are far more difficult than ours. They may be in hospitals, in prisons, in refugee camps, in war-torn countries; they may be hungry, crippled, and blind, without shelter or friends. Let this heart of compassion reach out to all of them; embrace them with it, empathize with them, realize their pain, wish to help.

Move your attention back to yourself, and let this feeling of compassion fill you from head to toe and surround you, giving you a sense of being helped and cared for, accepted, at ease.

May all beings have compassion for each other.

GUIDED LOVING-KINDNESS MEDITATION II

First, concentrate on the breath for just a moment.

Arouse in yourself the joy that comes from having the opportunity to practice this path, which brings the ultimate in peace, happiness, and complete fulfillment. Feel that joy within you, let it fill you, saturate you, and surround you.

Now feel joy with your neighbor in meditation, that he or she also has this great opportunity and is making use of it. Feel that joy for him or her and let it reach out to that person, filling and surrounding him or her with it.

Now feel that joy for everyone meditating with you, that everyone has this opportunity and is working hard to make it come alive. Let that joy reach out to everyone here, filling and surrounding him or her with it.

Think of your parents and have joy with them for all the things in their lives that they appreciate, whether you approve of them or not. Be joyful that they have some of the good things in life, and let that joy reach out to them, fill them and surround them with it.

Think of your nearest and dearest people, and have joy with their enjoyments, whatever they may be. Be joyful that they have pleasures and contentment, and let this joy reach out to them, fill them, and surround them.

Think of all your friends; have joy with their achievements, with anything that they are happy about. Feel the joy of their friendship; reach out to them with this joyful feeling to fill them and surround them with it.

Think of anyone whom you don't care for particularly, and let joy arise in your heart for that person's achievements, possessions, and accomplishments. Reach out to that person with joy, filling him or her with it, and embracing him or her with it.

Open up your heart wide and let joy flow out to as many people near and far as you can reach, being happy with their happiness, joyful with whatever they appreciate. Share your inner joy with them, filling them and surrounding them with it. Let it flow as far and wide as possible.

Now move your attention back to yourself, and let the joy in your heart fill you, saturate you, and give you new impetus and energy, because you realize the spiritual path is the most joyful endeavor. Let the happiness of having already accomplished some of the tasks on this path surround you, giving you the feeling of being safe and secure.

May all beings have joy in their hearts.

GUIDED LOVING-KINDNESS MEDITATION III

In order to begin, please put your attention on the breath for just a few moments.

Imagine that you have a beautiful white lotus flower growing in your heart and it is opening all its petals until it is fully open. Out of the center of the lotus flower in your heart comes a golden stream of light that fills you from head to toe with warmth and light and a feeling of contentment, and surrounds you with a feeling of lovingness and wellbeing.

Now let that golden stream of light from the center of your heart reach out to the person meditating nearest you and fill him or her with warmth and light and contentment. Surround him or her with lovingness and a sense of wellbeing.

Now open your heart wider, and enlarge this golden stream of light so that it can reach out to everyone with you in the room and fill them with warmth and light and a feeling of contentment. Surround everyone with your love and a sense of wellbeing as your gift.

Now think of your teachers, whether they are still alive or not, and let the golden stream of light from the center of your heart reach out to them and fill them with warmth and light and joy. Surround them with that golden stream of light, bringing them your love and a feeling of wellbeing.

Think of your parents, whether they are still alive or not. Let the golden stream of light from the center of your heart reach out to them, fill them with love and light, and surround them with warmth and with gratitude.

Think of those people who are nearest and dearest to you. Let the golden stream of light from the center of your heart reach out to them, fill them with your love, give them warmth and light, and surround them with a sense of wellbeing, without expecting them to return the same to you.

Think of all your good friends. Let the golden stream of light from the center of your heart reach out to all of them, fill them with the sincerity of your friendship, with your warmth, surround them with your love and with your care, without expecting them to return the same to you.

Think of all those people whom you encounter now and then, whether you know them or not: neighbors, people at work, people in the street, in the shops, people you meet while traveling. Let the golden stream of light enlarge and reach out to all of them, bringing your friendship and love to them, surrounding them with your care and concern, making them a real part of your life, which they actually are.

Think of anyone who may have made life difficult for you, who has put obstacles in your way, whom you find hard to love. Think of that person as your teacher. Let the golden stream of light from the center of your heart reach out to that person, so that no obstruction can remain in your own heart. Fill him or her with your gratitude for this opportunity of learning, with your acceptance and forgiveness, and surround him or her with love and compassion, realizing that everyone has the same pain and grief.

Think of all the people in your hometown. Open up your heart so wide that the golden stream of light can reach out to all the people there, enter into their houses, into their hearts, filling them with warmth and light and contentment, and surrounding them with your love and compassion, making them all part of your life, part of your heart.

Now turn your attention back to yourself, and let the golden stream of light fill you from head to toe with a feeling of joy and contentment, ease, and harmony within. Let it surround you with a feeling of wellbeing.

Now let the golden stream of light go back inside the lotus flower, which closes its petals. Then anchor the lotus flower in your heart, that the lotus may become one with your heart.

May all beings be happy.

The Buddha spoke of the many benefits we gain when we practice loving-kindness. The first three are that "one goes to sleep happily, one dreams no evil dreams, and one wakes happily." I hope you will go to sleep happily, dream no evil dreams, and wake happily.

FIVE DAILY RECOLLECTIONS: A GUIDED CONTEMPLATION

The Buddha recommended that every person should recollect five facts every day. They are well known to us, but we like to forget them. We like to pretend that they do not really exist. When they do happen, as they must, we think they are a tragedy, but they are nothing but laws of nature. This is a contemplation and not a meditation, and it is useful to know the difference between the two.

In meditation we try to focus and become one-pointed on the subject of meditation, so that the mind eventually becomes very calm and serene, and gains the power and strength to realize insights.

In contemplation, we take a subject that is a universal fact, not an individual problem, and see how it applies to us. We try to see how we react to that universality. Only our own reaction imbues the fact with importance for us.

Contemplation means that we stay with one subject, and although we have known the subject ever so long, a new realization may arise. We see the same thing in a different light. We experience an intuitive knowing, which comes from having discarded discursive thinking and from concentrating on one subject alone. This is how wisdom arises: not by thinking about a subject, but by contemplating its truth and realizing its application to our own life; seeing all its facets and connections to our reality, and gaining a brand new viewpoint.

We can compare that with looking at trees through a window from a sitting position and then standing up to look again. First we can only see half a tree, then we can see the whole of it. The tree has been whole all the time, but our own changed viewpoint has made the difference.

I'd like you to say each recollection aloud, which will help you to memorize it. After the sentence I will add something to help with the contemplation. You need not use what I am suggesting, because these are only aids to give a guideline and direction. If you have other ideas, that is very good. To contemplate one's own insights has more impact.

First, put the attention on the breath for just a moment. Now, please say this sentence:

I AM OF THE NATURE TO DECAY. I HAVE NOT GONE BEYOND DECAY.

The first consideration is to ascertain whether this is true, and if so, whether we have actually paid attention to it in our lives. Then we can investigate whether there is any kind of resistance to it in our minds, whether we would rather not have it happen. If that is so, then we need to find out why we do not like this law of nature.

I AM OF THE NATURE TO BE DISEASED. I HAVE NOT GONE BEYOND DISEASE.

Again we can inquire whether this is true, whether we've had sicknesses, and whether we can expect this body to have them again. It is useful to find out what this tells us about our body, which we are used to calling "me." Does our body really obey our wishes? Or does it have its own nature and become sick without our wish and our will?

I AM OF THE NATURE TO DIE. I HAVE NOT GONE BEYOND DEATH.

We all know this is true. But we need to think about whether we are keeping in mind that this may happen at any time, and whether we are living accordingly. We may ask ourselves if we are ready, and if not, what is holding us back. And what are we doing about getting ready, so that death is not a threat?

ALL THAT IS MINE, DEAR, AND DELIGHTFUL WILL CHANGE AND VANISH.

By remembering incidents of the past, we can recollect whether things, experiences, situations, and people that we held dear and found delightful have changed and/or vanished. If they have, what about all we deem dear and delightful now? Will it remain with us?

THE FIFTH RECOLLECTION: KARMA

I AM THE OWNER OF MY KARMA.

When we accept this fact, we are starting to take responsibility for all that happens to us. We need to contemplate whether we are really owning our karma and drop the belief that others have created anything at all for us.

I AM HEIR TO MY KARMA.

Each of us manufactures our own inheritance. If we keep that in mind, and recollect it often, we will find it easier to do only that which is wholesome and useful.

I AM BORN OF MY KARMA.

Our own wish to be here and to be alive brought us into the circumstances of our birth. That situation is meant for us as a learning experience.

I AM RELATED TO MY KARMA.

Here we can contemplate that this is the closest relationship we will ever have, as close as our own skin. It is the one we have to come to terms with and the one we need to accept.

WHATEVER KARMA I SHALL CREATE, WHETHER GOOD OR EVIL, THAT I SHALL INHERIT.

This brings us to this present moment, realizing that karma is being made by us almost constantly, and that our inheritance is often immediate and of our own making.

4 Dependent Arising: Cause and Effect

THE TEACHING OF THE BUDDHA can be called a teaching of cause and effect, since these play an important part in his expositions of the Dhamma. The word Dhamma means, literally translated, "law" or "law of nature." So when he expounds Dhamma, he describes the law of nature, of which cause and effect form an integral part.

The Buddha did not teach Buddhism. That is a later designation. He described his teaching as Dhamma. He said, "Who sees dependent arising, sees Dhamma. Who sees Dhamma, sees dependent arising." "Seeing" means in-seeing, within oneself, and "dependent arising" denotes cause and effect. The Buddha gave two separate teachings on cause and effect.[2] Both have great application to our lives, and if we not only understand them but also use them, we will find our lives flow much more harmoniously.

We also need to remember again and again that meditation taken out of context cannot succeed. It may bring some peacefulness eventually, but it will not bring the real transformation that a spiritual path provides. Meditation is a means to sharpen, strengthen, and calm the mind, and is not an end in itself. It is the one thing we can do to get our mind in shape. But then we have to make use of it for its intended purpose, which is our growth process in thoughts and emotions. Eventually, we will have a totally mature mind that has no obstructions in it.

The Buddha gave his initial explanation of dependent arising in the form of a picture that he drew in the sand for his monks as a teaching aid. The monks were so delighted with this that they asked permission to reproduce the picture. The Buddha agreed and stipulated that a copy was to be hung in every monastery, where one person was to be designated an expert in explaining it, so that any visitor could learn the meaning of dependent arising in this manner. The monasteries and most of the artifacts of the Buddha's time were destroyed in India by the Muslim invasion, yet the knowledge of this drawing was transmitted to Tibet, where even today it is still available to us, in an artistically elaborate and detailed version. In the Buddha's time, it would have been far more simply executed.

When we examine this picture, we find a large circle or wheel with a stylized tiger on top hanging on to the outer rim. His large tail hangs below the wheel, and on his head is a diadem of five skulls, which symbolize the five aspects of a human being, termed the five aggregates (*khandha*s). The tiger is depicted as a creature of some beauty; he has curls on his head and bracelets on his claws, and even rings on his toes—but he still looks as ferocious as any tiger. His mouth is wide open, apparently trying to swallow the wheel. He manifests impermanence; no matter how nicely we dress it up by beautifying ourselves, impermanence still swallows us totally anyway.

Inside the wheel there is a small circle, a centerpiece containing three animals: a snake, a cock, and a pig, which bite each other's tails and thereby form an inner circle. The snake is symbolic of hate, because it carries poison within. The cock represents greed, because it has a whole barnyard full of hens. The pig signifies delusion, because when it throws dirt over its head, it can't see anything at all. These three demonstrate the unwholesome roots that are our birthright—delusion being the underlying factor, and greed and hate the two resulting tendencies.

If we accept the fact that we ourselves sometimes lack wisdom and often want or reject something, we can become more tolerant and accepting of ourselves and others, no matter who they are. Some may have jurisdiction over a whole country, some may even be able to declare war; others may be just those people we live with. Everybody is beset by greed, hate, and delusion, including ourselves. Only the enlightened one has done away with these defilements. With some introspection we can easily detect them within ourselves, particularly greed and hate. Delusion is harder to recognize, because it takes wisdom to find it. Greed and hate need not be thought of as violence or passion. They arise with everything we like and dislike. Whatever we want or reject, both are greed and hate. When we see that in ourselves, we can realize it as the human dilemma. Only when we do that will we use our power of recognition and our emotional tolerance in the right way. There are grades of distinction between people, but they are only subtle differences. The real change comes when there has been liberation, freedom.

Enclosing the three animals is a bigger circle, usually divided into six parts, depicting the six realms of existence. One is the human realm, and it is entirely up to the artist what is shown there: mothers with babies, workers in the rice fields, machinery, and vehicles. Sometimes there is also a war going on in that picture. Next is the animal realm, showing many different species. Following that we usually find a representation of hell, which is a state of depraved consciousness. Whatever the artist's imagination allows is pictured here: raging fires, tortures, floods, and famine are endured by unfortunate beings. Next is the realm of the hungry ghosts. These are portrayed as having very tiny throats and mouths but huge bellies that can never be filled. Their greed has been so great that it can never be satisfied, which is another low state of consciousness. Then there are the *asura*s, who are always fighting, living in a constant state of war and aggression. These are the four realms lower than the human realm. There's also the *deva* realm, possibly comparable to heaven, paradise, or utopia, depicted as a beautiful abode with lovely beings surrounded by flowers and butterflies in exquisite colors. These different states of consciousness can be experienced by all of us in this one lifetime.

The outer rim of the wheel is the most important one. It is divided into twelve parts. The first picture is of an old, blind woman with a stick trying to find her way through a dense forest. This represents our ignorance. In Buddhist terminology, ignorance does not mean lack of schooling, but rather ignoring the laws of nature. Since we are ignoring the laws of nature within ourselves, we also do so in our environment. Therefore we have dying forests, contaminated rivers, polluted air, and all sorts of natural catastrophes, which we ourselves have brought about. Our surroundings are subject to the same rules as we are, namely the law of change, of impermanence, and of nonsubstantiality, "corelessness." But since we ignore these truths, we cannot live according to them and are actually trying to defy them. This is the root of all our problems.

We can think of ignorance as a beginningless beginning. When people asked the Buddha about the beginning of the universe, he never answered. That was one of the "four imponderables"[3] on which he did not wish to elaborate. He pointed to ignorance as the cause of our problems. When total liberation (*nibbāna*) is reached, one knows the answers to all the questions anyway, and until then it is only necessary to practice to reach that state.

That whole circle always depicts cause and effect. The next picture shows a potter making pots. He has some pretty, well-shaped pots and also some broken ones. This is symbolic of our karma-making. Because we are beset with this "me" and "mine" delusion, we make karma, good, bad, and neutral. Initially karma is mind-made, since we start everything with the thinking process. This is why it is so important to meditate, to train the mind, and also to know something about the Buddha's teaching, to help us make enough good karma for our options to remain open. If we make enough bad karma, we can end up in prison; on the other hand, with enough good karma we can live with a consciousness where our inner being is at ease, loving, and compassionate.

So we need to remember that karma is always initiated in the mind and then followed up by speech and action. We only have these three doors: thought, speech, and action. Since all starts in the mind, that's our first and foremost focus of attention. Meditation is the means by which the mind can be made sharp, clear, and insightful enough for us to change from the negative to the positive. We don't have to carry on with thinking negative thoughts; it's totally unnecessary.

Due to having created karma, rebirth consciousness arises. But we need not think of rebirth only as a future life. We are, in actual fact, reborn every moment with new thoughts and feelings, and we bring with us the karma that we made in past moments. If we were angry a moment ago, we are not going to feel good immediately. If we were loving a moment ago, we would be feeling fine now. Thus we live from moment to moment with the results of our karma.

Every morning, particularly, can be seen as a rebirth. The day is young, we are full of energy, and we have a whole day ahead of us. Every moment we get older, and are tired enough in the evening to fall asleep and die a small death. All we can do then is toss and turn in bed, with our mind dreamy and foggy. Every day can be regarded as a whole life span, since we can only live one day at a time; the past is gone and the future may or may not come; only this rebirth, this day, this moment, is important.

Rebirth consciousness contains the karma we have accumulated. What went on lifetimes ago, when we might have been a Persian dancer, an Egyptian princess, or a Viking warrior, or whatever else we think we were, is totally immaterial, isn't it? It's often fantasy. What is truly important is the here and now, this one day that can actually be lived. When we realize we bring our karma with us, it might induce us to use that one day to the best of our ability, not frittering the time away, or using it in useless pursuits, but paying attention to our spiritual growth.

The rebirth consciousness can be likened to a monkey hopping from tree to tree (from life to life), because an untrained mind is not capable of staying on one subject without digressing and lacks one-pointed direction. We can compare that to our states of mind during the day. There are certain things that we are probably forced to do because we have to earn a living, look after a family, or attend to other responsibilities, but a spiritual direction is often missing. If we consider our rebirth every morning with a feeling of gratitude in the heart, that here is another day during which we do not have to go hungry or be without shelter, but have the opportunity to practice, our good karma-making will stand a much better chance.

Due to rebirth consciousness, mind and body arise. If we carry our analogy of rebirth every morning a little further, we can say that when we wake up, we know that we have mind and body. While we are fast asleep, nothing really tells us who we are. Our first step into insight will necessitate the understanding that mind and body are two. The idea that this is "me," one complete whole, and that all is happening because "I" need, want, or feel it, is erroneous. That takes personal choice away, as well as the possibility of making good karma, and negates the spiritual life. Spiritual life can only have reality when we know that we can fashion what we want in life with our minds, and that the body is our servant. Some bodies are better servants than others, and it doesn't hurt to make our own servant into a good one by any means that we can find, such as food, exercise, or medicine. But it remains the servant; the master is the mind. Imagine for a moment having a body here in front of us that has no mind and hacking that body to pieces. It won't object; there's nothing there that can object. We can do what we like with it. But put a mind into the body and we have a different situation.

The usual picture for this sequence is a boat with a prone passenger and a boatman who is paddling. The passenger is the body, and the boatman is the mind. We cannot do anything without the mind telling us to do it. If our mind hadn't told us to meditate, our body wouldn't be sitting down to do so. The mind is very much affected by the aches and pains of the body, but only because it is untrained. The Buddha's and the enlightened ones' minds are no longer affected by the unpleasant feelings in the body. In fact, unpleasantness of the body is unavoidable. Everyone has some sort of sickness once in a while, or some aches and pains. Unless we die young, we will grow old, and older bodies don't function as well as young ones. The Buddha said, "The untrained, unenlightened disciple has two darts, two arrows that pierce him. The trained, enlightened disciple has one." The two darts that pierce us are mind and body. Both give us unpleasant experiences. But the enlightened disciple only has the body to contend with. The mind no longer reacts. The Buddha also became sick during his lifetime and contracted an illness that led to his death, yet he was able to go into the meditative absorptions on his deathbed because his mind was not affected by bodily discomfort.

In our case, of course, the mind is affected by the body and reacts to it. But eventually we will be able to separate the two when we have gained enough skill in meditation and insight. We will understand what is mind and what is body, and realize that it is the mind that needs the most attention, although we usually act just the opposite way. Most of our time and energy are spent on the body. We look after its nourishment, wash it and clean it, exercise it, rest it in bed at night, and shelter it in our home. We clothe it for warmth and protection, and if it should become sick, we obtain medicine.

The mind needs at least as much as, or even more of this kind of attention than the body. Obviously it needs to rest. The only way it can ever do so is to stop thinking and experience calm and peace. At night when the body rests, the mind dreams, and during the day, it thinks. We are overworking the finest, most delicate, most valuable tool that exists in the universe. Then we are surprised that things don't work out the way we thought they should, and that the world we live in is not the kind of paradise it ought to be. The minds that fashion the world we live in, including our own, cannot function at full capacity, because they are totally overworked. They have not had a rest, a cleanup, or any necessary medicine. Such minds are running downhill instead of regenerating. Meditation is our way of regenerating the mind.

One moment of concentration is one moment of purification, which constitutes the cleanup. Calm and peace give the mind its needed rest, and knowing and remembering the Dhamma is the medicine for all our fears, worries, hates, and delusions. Looking after the mind does not mean stuffing more knowledge into it, but rather understanding with wisdom, which can make us completely well, so there never needs to be any delusion again. Naturally it is a progressive and gradual pathway, but at least we can be aware of what can be done. When we realize that the mind is the one paddling the boat, with the body as a passenger, then we have a much better insight into our priorities.

The next picture shows a house with five windows and a door, symbolizing our five senses. The door, representing the capacity to think, allows entry to all and sundry if it is not guarded. This is an important point to understand and remember. Each person has six openings to the world, and when we use only those, we will always know the world in the same limited way, through seeing, hearing, tasting, touching, smelling, and thinking. As long as we remain unaware of anything else, we shall keep looking for fulfillment in the wrong direction. Our sense contacts, including thinking, can never keep their promise to satisfy. They are doomed to constant change.

As long as we fail to realize that we have to go beyond the sensual aspect of ourselves, we will look in vain for satisfaction, not only because all our sense contacts are bound to be both pleasant and unpleasant, but also because they are necessarily short-lived. They must not last under any circumstances.

Can you imagine listening to Beethoven's Ninth Symphony for three days in a row, hearing just that from morning to night? After a while it would no longer be pleasurable, and we would probably refuse ever to listen to it again. The same goes for eating. Let us imagine that we have had a very nice meal, and we tell our host that we liked it very much. Then our host says, "I'm glad you liked it. I've plenty of food here; please stay another two or three hours and eat some more." If we were to do that, we would be in utter misery. A pleasurable meal can last half an hour or so at the most. The same goes for all our sense contacts. They have to be short-lived. We cannot listen, eat, touch, or look for long periods of time. If any of our sense contacts last too long, they turn into an utter disaster for us. Even the most pleasant sense contact cannot last. They are constantly disappearing, so that we have to find new ones.

Our economy runs on that principle. We can't sell people anything that doesn't provide pleasant feelings, so everything is geared toward that single purpose. Since pleasure has a very short life span, we spend time, energy, thought, and attention on its recurrence. But fulfillment cannot come about in that way. It is all just momentary pleasure, and whether we admit that or not, we know it as an underlying truth. Often that becomes the reason for wanting to try meditation. Yet we need a fair bit of determination and absolute steadiness in the practice.

The next picture in this sequence shows the sense contact, depicted as a man and woman embracing. The symbolism is that as long as our senses are functioning, they make contact, and our preference is for the pleasant ones, which we constantly desire. If we have eyes that function, we see; if we have ears that function, we hear; if we have taste buds, we taste; if we have a body, we touch; and if we have a mind, ideas arise and thinking starts, all of it happening automatically. There's nothing to say that it shouldn't be that way. But we need a little more insight into what makes us tick so that we can gain some control over our lives.

As long as there are senses, we make contact. This becomes very apparent in the sitting position in meditation. From our continual touch contact an unpleasant feeling eventually arises. This is a natural sequence of human events. But there is a step in this progression that doesn't have to be automatically preprogrammed.

The next picture shows a man who is having arrows shot into his eyes, a very unpleasant feeling, to say the least. But there is no way we can avoid the arising of feeling after a sense contact; even an enlightened person makes sense contacts and has feelings. However, the next step can be the doorway out of the wheel of birth and death.

We move from feeling to craving, and the next picture usually shows a person sitting at a laden banquet table, shoveling food into himself. Craving does not only mean wanting to get something, it can also mean wanting to get rid of something. In the case of our own touch contact in sitting, we want to get rid of unpleasant feelings by moving the body. That is the craving that keeps us in the ever-recurring cycle of trying to escape from unpleasant feelings and wanting only pleasant ones, a cycle that we have all been repeating for years on end.

The cyclic nature of our existence can only be interrupted at this point, when feeling is understood to be just feeling, without our owning it. If it were our own, why would we be getting unpleasant feelings? It would be utterly foolish to choose unpleasant ones. If we had any say in the matter, we would naturally have only pleasant feelings. If feelings really belonged to us, we would of course throw the unpleasant ones away and keep only the pleasant ones. But nobody is capable of doing that. Everybody has both pleasant and unpleasant feelings. In this case, feelings encompass physical sensations and emotions.

This doorway leading out of our preprogrammed round of birth and death is accessible to us when insight arises to the degree where we no longer reject and resist, when we have understood and experienced that things are as they are, namely a constant flow and nothing more. We need only be aware of this perpetual movement, to watch it, know it, but not to put ourselves in the middle of it by wanting what is pleasant or getting rid of what is unpleasant. In other words, we practice equanimity, even-mindedness.

Equanimity is one of the seven factors of enlightenment,[4] and we all have the capacity to practice it, especially when we realize that unpleasant feelings just exist. We believe we have some jurisdiction over them because of their arising and ceasing. Naturally we wish to hasten their departure, sometimes even with aspirin or by stronger means. In meditation we do it by moving our sitting position. All this gives rise to the illusion that we are in control of our feelings, but we are actually only disguising the law of nature. We are putting a cover over it so that we don't have to look at it too closely. One day when we take an honest look at the law of nature as it really is, we will see that all our beliefs are fantasies. Hopefully we will at least smile at ourselves, if not laugh. Since there is so much to cover up all the time, our energy is dissipated and fulfillment evades us. However, what is real and true will be reflected in our lives again and again, so that we will continually find ourselves trying to cover up and disguise what we don't like, unless we are willing to accept reality.

By practicing letting go of our reactions we can find the doorway out. Each time we fail to respond to something, we have taken a big step toward freedom. Until we have done that, we are constant victims of our feelings, which is not pleasant at all. Because we can run away, we are deluded into thinking we are in charge, but unpleasant feelings always resurface. When we are still the victim of our pleasant and unpleasant feelings, wanting the one and rejecting the other, we are not master of our own lives. When we learn to let go of unpleasant feelings, paying no attention to them, accepting them as just feelings, we become master of the situation for that moment. We gain confidence that it is possible to be unaffected and non-reacting. Inner power arises from that certitude. This is not power over others but power over oneself, which helps us to see clearly into absolute reality.

But if we bypass that doorway by reacting once again to our feelings, we reenter the automatic progression of cause and effect. The next step is clinging, usually depicted by a person picking fruit off a tree and throwing it into baskets that are already full to overflowing. It's actually not a bad symbol for the kind of agricultural mess we encounter these days in the affluent countries, where tons of butter are going to waste, and surplus coffee is being dumped in the ocean. But the intended meaning of the picture is that our grasping is so strong that we don't even notice when we already have enough. As soon as we crave anything, we are already clinging to our desires, thereby undermining our peace of mind. Subconsciously we realize that whatever we crave—person or object—is impermanent, about to change, and subject to deterioration, theft, or loss. Although we know all that, we don't want to acknowledge these facts. However, because we do know, a feeling of fear accompanies all clinging: the fear of loss.

We can recognize this clearly with belongings. Rich people often have burglar alarms, double locks, ferocious dogs, huge fences, and large insurance policies. They are afraid their belongings will be stolen, burned in a fire, or claimed by outsiders. Fears about losing beloved people often result in jealousy, a most unpleasant emotion.

When we have missed our chance of releasing ourselves from suffering because we have reacted once again to feelings, we are already committed to clinging to whatever it may be that we either desire or reject. No matter how trivial that may be, a certain anxiety will arise.

The Buddha said, "The way to liberation is the way of letting go of clinging." "Letting go" is our spiritual growth process. There's nothing to gain, nothing to get. In order to meditate we have to let go of all sensual desires, no matter how subtle. If we don't let go of hopes, ideas, thoughts, worries, and problems during our meditation periods, we can't concentrate. "Letting go" is the key phrase for the spiritual path. Knowing that all is impermanent, cannot last, and is moving toward dissolution helps us to let go. Wanting always results in anxiety, because we don't know whether we will get what we desire, and even if we do, we don't know whether we can keep it.

From clinging arises the idea of "becoming." We could relate the whole circle to this one lifetime. We don't have to think of future and past lives at all, although this progression is often explained as occurring over three lifetimes. In this case, the past life encompasses ignorance and the karma formations, which are the first two steps of cause and effect shown in the Buddha's explanation of our cyclic involvement with life and death. The arising of rebirth consciousness in the womb in this lifetime results in future becoming, unless we find the doorway leading out. But we can experience the whole cycle in this one lifetime, which is even more useful, because we are concerned with what is happening to us right now. Past lives are gone and there is little, if anything, we can do about them; they have disappeared down the ages. Future ones are conjecture. So we had better attend to essentials now.

Becoming, which results from clinging, involves the idea of having or being something more satisfying than at present. We want to become a very good meditator, or we want to become spiritual, or more learned. We have all sorts of ideas but all are bound up with wanting to become, because we are not satisfied with what we are. Often we do not even pay attention to what we are now but just know that something is lacking. Instead of trying to realize what we are and investigating where the difficulty actually lies, we just dream of becoming something else. When we have become something or someone else, we can be just as dissatisfied as before. If we have lived in the city, for example, we might move to the country and take up farming. For a while we are delighted. When the novelty wears off, we move back to the city and get a job in an office, and again dissatisfaction sets in. Becoming is never going to satisfy us.

Investigation and insight into who we really are is the answer. When we get down to rock bottom, we will see that it doesn't matter what we become; we are essentially always the same. We will understand that what we really are will never change because it is something entirely different from what we think we are.

Becoming is fraught with difficulty, because it is a reaching out toward something we may or may not accomplish. It is concerned with getting away from what we are now and going toward something we want in the future. There's no peace to be found in this; rather it is full of restlessness. The symbolic picture for becoming usually shows a pregnant woman with a baby growing in her, because that is the ultimate becoming. Because we don't see the futility and the emptiness of what we have been doing and what life is all about, we want to become again.

We want to be here. We do not wish to give it all up. We want to be somebody, and this wanting results in our being born. We could again use the analogy of being born each morning to good advantage. The related picture is of a baby at birth, or in a baby carriage, or being carried on someone's back.

The following picture is often of an old man with a sack of bones on his back, symbolizing death. We find written under the picture, "And this is how this whole mass of suffering arises." From ignorance, through craving and clinging, to becoming. This can give us a good indication also why things happen in our lives the way they do. Our own wanting or our own rejections are the triggers. The stronger our desires, the stronger our experiences.

QUESTIONS

STUDENT: *How does ego delusion apply to our wanting to make good karma?*

AYYA KHEMA: As long as we have ego delusion, there is always wanting. There's no possibility of not having it. So when there is the ego delusion, the only way is to make wise choices, even though all choices are "wanting."

Only the fully enlightened one has fully realized emptiness and therefore doesn't make any more karma. But for us, it is essential that we discriminate between wise and unwise choices, so that we make good karma. It certainly concerns our own wanting, which is our direction in life. The step out of the whole of our suffering is nonreaction. Not necessarily the actions we take, but rather letting go of our preprogrammed reactions.

S: *When we do the contemplation acknowledging that we are going to die, you said we also have to live accordingly. Could you elaborate on that?*

AK: The contemplation we undertook earlier is called the five daily recollections. The Buddha recommended that every person should remember every single day that we are not here forever. This is a guest performance, which can be finished any time. We have no idea when. We always think that we may have seventy-five or eighty years to live, but who knows? If we remember our vulnerability every single day, our lives will be imbued with the understanding that each moment counts, and we will not be so concerned with the future. Now is the time to grow on the spiritual path. If we remember that, we will also have a different relationship to the people around us. They too can die at any moment, and we certainly wouldn't like that to happen at a time when we are not loving toward them. When we remember that, our practice connects to this moment, and meditation improves because there is urgency behind it. We need to act now. We can only watch this one breath, not the next one.

S: *I often find it difficult to live an ordinary life and relate to my friends while practicing at the same time.*

AK: Actually, practicing is quite ordinary. The Zen people have a lovely saying: "Nothing special." As one continues to meditate and tries to purify one's emotions and reactions, one finds it simpler to relate to people and often feels that every confrontation is a welcome challenge to exercise love and compassion. The more one recognizes the suffering in one's own heart, and has compassion for one's own struggle, the easier it becomes to recognize the same in everyone else and respond with compassion.

Our ordinary, everyday activities offer us unlimited opportunities for mindfulness, and they are therefore our base for practice (in Pali, *kammaṭṭhāna*—our spheres of action or subjects of mental training).

When our inner life changes, the outer life often follows suit. At first this may be imperceptible, but eventually both become harmonious and integrated.

S: *How can one actually let go of pain in the sitting position?*

AK: Letting go is a state of mind that makes it possible to let go of all resistance in the body, eliminating pain. In the beginning that will naturally be only momentary. Pain and aversion will then arise again, and one should not allow aversion to take a hold. It doesn't help our practice. All that remains then is to change the sitting position. One has to assess one's own capacity and just go a little further than one has been able to do before. It's impossible to jump over our own shadow, but it is very helpful to experience what it feels like to let go of an unpleasant feeling by having our attention riveted to something else. The unpleasant feeling doesn't exist in our consciousness at that time. That's an occasion for meaningful insight, because it becomes clear that we only know whatever direction our consciousness takes.

S: *Is it easier to be a spiritual person when living as a nun or a monk, with more time for meditation, than when leading an ordinary life?*

AK: It's impossible to say, because some meditators may have already practiced much in past lives. If one wants to lead a spiritual life, it does not depend on meditation alone, sitting quietly on a pillow, secluded from everything else. A spiritual life is lived in the world. It isn't only what one does, it's mainly how one does it. One can be totally removed from spirituality in a nunnery, I can assure you, and yet meditate every morning and evening. It is a matter of how we approach every action, every experience—whether we can actually use difficulties as challenges and not get angry, worried, fearful, or envious, but accept situations as our own learning experiences, every day, every moment in our lives. The more we are in the world, the more confrontations we have, and these are often the causes of negative reactions. To learn to change our negative reactions to loving-kindness and compassion is the great purifier in daily life. It doesn't matter where we are; we can do that anywhere. Much better in the middle of the biggest crowd than sitting all alone in a cave.

S: *How does one decide to become a monk or nun?*

AK: It usually decides itself. If it doesn't do that, it could easily be wrong. It isn't like a big turnabout. I think you can compare it with the decision to get married or not. How do people decide? I don't know. It's just a progressive step that one takes when that appears to be the right thing in one's life.

S: *Is the experience of oneness comparable to enlightenment?*

AK: No, absolutely not. A totality experience can be a meditative stage, but it is certainly not enlightenment. To become one with something else one still has to be there, and that is not the final act. Liberation is also a law of nature. I don't know whether it's useful to discuss something that is still nebulous at this moment, but we could say one thing: both the enlightened and the unenlightened states are in our own mind. There's nothing else to become enlightened except the mind. Because both states are available to us, they are both laws of nature. The unenlightened state is a state of consciousness in which latent desires cover up our inherent purity. When we are able to let go of all impurities completely, then the enlightened state becomes evident in the mind. Both states can be found in exactly the same spot, except for the fact that we are lacking the awareness to realize this.

5 Transcendental Dependent Arising: Unsatisfactoriness

STEP 1

THE TEACHING OF DEPENDENT ARISING is the centerpiece of the Buddha's Dhamma and shows us the causes and effects that exist within and outside of us. There are two separate and distinct teachings of dependent arising. The one that is more widely known is called the worldly dependent arising (*lokiya paticca samuppāda*). It concerns the wheel of birth and death, which starts out with ignorance and goes through the cycle of three lives—past, present, and future—from ignorance to renewed birth and death. Within that cycle there is one doorway through which we can step out, namely, the space between feeling and craving. All the other steps of dependent arising are automatic causes and effects. Unless we learn to live with unpleasant and pleasant feelings, without wanting to get rid of the one or keeping and renewing the other, we don't have access to that doorway—we continue to circle around the wheel of birth and death over and over again. Our training leads us to equanimity as the pinnacle of all emotions, so that our feelings no longer get the better of us. As long as we are victims of our feelings and our emotions, we are not really free. The Buddha's teaching directs us to freedom, which includes being independent. Within our thought processes we generate our karma, so we have to watch our thoughts and not take them for granted.

Meditation is all about becoming master of the mind, so that the mind will no longer play games with us. As long as we have no control over its formations, our karma will always be a mixture of wholesome and unwholesome. Because craving will enter our mind innumerable times, we will again and again experience unsatisfactoriness, which the Buddha expounded as the first and second noble truths, namely, "There is unsatisfactoriness" and "It has only one cause—craving." Unsatisfactoriness makes our lives unfulfilled, which causes us to search for some transcending reality.

Therefore the Buddha showed us the chain of cause and effect of transcendental dependent arising (*lokuttara paticca samuppāda*), which does not move in a circle. Instead, it operates in a straight line from our present state to the enlightened state. Dependent arising drawn in a circular manner shows us quite clearly that we are caught in a net of karmic resultants.

In transcendental dependent arising, the Buddha explains in a succession of twelve steps how to get from this worldly existence to liberation. The whole of the Buddha's teaching, and the sole purpose of meditation in the Buddha's dispensation, is elevating our worldly, everyday, consciousness to liberation. Liberation is a state of mind, available to all of us (otherwise we need not practice), but covered over and hidden by our desires. In our tradition, the candles we put on a shrine are the symbol for enlightened mind.

If we didn't have that potential within us, forty-five years of teaching by the Buddha would have been in vain. After his enlightenment under the bodhi tree,[5] the Buddha first enjoyed the bliss of liberation by himself. After a month he considered spreading this news to others, but it occurred to him that people would not be able to grasp the profundity of this absolute truth, and that would be a vexation to him. Tradition tells us that the highest *brahma* of the god realms, named Sahampati, came to beg the Buddha to teach for the benefit of gods and humans. The Buddha applied his divine vision and saw that there were some people who had little dust in their eyes, in their inner perception, and therefore decided to teach.

There are and always have been those who can use the Buddha's words to reach liberation. We have today the same problems, the same potential and solidity, that people have always had. Everything that we do in the Buddha's dispensation has liberation as its goal, its purpose. We need to keep in mind that we must constantly let go of all that covers our enlightened mind. Transcendental dependent arising begins where worldly dependent arising ends, namely with suffering.

Suffering does not just mean tragedy, or necessarily pain, or even being unhappy. It encompasses all of that, yet it is more far reaching. That is why this Pali word can hardly be properly translated; it contains far too many possibilities. The fundamental meaning of unsatisfactoriness is our inability to find total satisfaction anywhere within existence. Only when we have understood that will we no longer suffer.

While we are still searching for satisfaction within worldly existence—from other people's appreciation or kindness, from good situations, from our knowledge, or our own goodness—we will eventually be disappointed, for the simple reason of impermanence. Impermanence (*anicca*), unsatisfactoriness (*dukkha*), and corelessness (*anattā*) are the three characteristics of the whole of existence. As long as we have the idea that there is something to be found in the world that can make us permanently and totally happy, we leave ourselves wide open to unhappiness. Since it cannot be found, we have a valid reason for not being happy. We look here and there, move from one place to another, change our partner, our diet, our religion, our method of meditation, our exercises, and what happens? Usually nothing but dissatisfaction again. In Pali, this search is called *papañca*, which means proliferation. Nature itself contains enormous variety. Think of the number of species of trees, birds, flowers, and insects, the different colors to be found everywhere, the variability in people. None of us look alike and yet we are all human beings.

Nature proliferates, and as long as we go along with that, we are looking for something other than what we have. This alone is unsatisfactoriness. It means that there is an emptiness within that wants to be filled. Unless we see this quite clearly, we will always try to fill this void from outside, through our sense contacts. But it can't be done that way; only when we realize we must fulfill ourselves from within can we begin to take the spiritual path.

As long as we have not seen this clearly, suffering will cause us to react in one of the many popular ways available to us. The first one is often to blame someone else. This is very popular and appears to be an easy way out of any problem. It doesn't work at all, however, because that particular suffering not having been dealt with, it will arise again and again. Our whole sojourn in this life is like an adult education class, and if we don't manage to pass the exams, we have to go through the same class again, just as in any school. The suffering we have not conquered will confront us as another exam.

Another popular way to respond to suffering is to run away from it. We don't even have to physically remove ourselves, although that, too, is common. We can use books, radio, television, movies, or discussions to drown any self-perception.

Another reaction to suffering is self-pity, which is fairly widespread but quite useless and counterproductive, since it generates more unhappiness. Once self-pity has set in, the next step is near at hand, namely, depression. Some people actually hang on to their suffering and want to keep it. Any advice on how to eliminate it is not well received, and why is that? Because people feel alive with their suffering; they own it, which produces a sense of emotional plenitude, even though negatively.

Suffering is our best teacher. It will not be persuaded by any pleading of misery to let go of us. If we say to a human teacher, "I don't feel well," "My back aches," "I can't get up in the morning," "I'd rather go home," the teacher may reply, "I am very sorry, but if you want to go home, then you must go." If we say to suffering, "Look, I don't feel well," "My back aches," "I want to go home," suffering says, "That's fine, but I am coming along." There is no way to say goodbye to it unless and until we have transcended our reactions. This means that we have looked suffering squarely in the eye and have seen it for what it is—a universal characteristic of existence and nothing else. The reason we are fooled is that because this life contains so many pleasant occasions and sense contacts, we think if we could just keep this pleasantness going suffering would never come again. We try over and over again to make this happen, until in the end we finally see that the pleasantness cannot continue because the law of impermanence intervenes. Yet the whole of human society is built on just that concept—that it must be possible to perpetuate pleasantness. So we continue our search for something new, because everybody else is doing it, too.

We forget that pleasantness is due to sense contact and therefore has to be impermanent; otherwise, it will become most unpleasant, whether it is taste, touch, sight, sound, smell, or thought. Some contacts last a little longer, but all of them have to end before they become utter misery. Yet we rely on these contacts to make our lives pleasant and happy. After having tried this so many times, it must finally come to our attention that not only are the sense contacts impermanent, but even when most pleasant, they leave something to be desired. There is no total satisfaction to be found in them, and that is unsatisfactoriness.

This practice may bring us to the point where we think we may be able to find fulfillment on the spiritual path. But even that may go astray if we don't accept that there, too, suffering is experienced until the point at which we have transcended it all. The Buddha said there were four kinds of people on a spiritual path. One group has a lot of suffering and it takes them a long time to achieve any results. Another group has a lot of suffering, but they can achieve results very quickly. Another group has a lot of pleasant feelings, and it takes them a long time to achieve results. There is one group of people who have a lot of pleasant feelings and who achieve quick results, but if we don't belong to that group, we have to expect and tolerate unsatisfactory conditions arising in this existence.

Liberation goes beyond personal existence, but within personal existence, unsatisfactoriness is. If we accept that fully, we don't have to suffer. This is the most important aspect of understanding unsatisfactoriness. Once that insight has penetrated our lives, we are able to forge ahead and experience much happiness on the spiritual path. That unsatisfactoriness exists physically is a well-known fact. Even the Buddha had physical pain. Bodily pain is a given, but we react with the mind, so that when the body hurts, the mind hurts with it. Even enlightened ones cannot stop the body's pains, but the mind's reaction can be stopped. The body is so fragile and so prone to decay, disease, and death that there is always something wrong with it, whether it is old age or just a cold, backache, or toothache. We have to constantly look after the body, but the mind does not have to be affected by that at all.

In the realm of unsatisfactoriness we also need to accept that our bodies will never quite give satisfaction. Older people find that easy to accept. It is more difficult for the young. The Buddha called that the "intoxication with youth," and Bernard Shaw said that "Youth is wasted on the young."

The body needs constant care and attention because it is always falling apart. Once we see that as part of this whole suffering existence, we may get an inkling that it might be better not to be reborn in such a body. When that inkling happens, urgency (*saṃvega*) follows, namely the urgency to practice. The body has to have food, which means having to eat, digest, and excrete constantly. It has to be looked after with regard to cleanliness, rest, the neat appearance of nails, hair, skin, and teeth, and it must be provided with medicine when needed. There is a constant bother about the body. It is hardly possible to say that this body gives pleasure.

When one is very young, this is difficult to see because the body is still very strong, without aches and pains. But imagine for just one minute that you were sitting in meditation without a body. Wouldn't that be far easier? Maybe that brings the idea home how difficult it is to have a human body.

However, the Buddha said that the human realm is the best realm in which to gain enlightenment, because we have plenty of pain—particularly with the body—to spur us on. Yet we also have pleasure, creating a balance that makes it possible for us to practice. In the realms lower than human, the pain is so great that practice is almost impossible. In the realms above us, pleasure is so prevalent that the urgency to practice disappears. There are always *deva*s around who are practicing, but they are a minority. Of course, with humans it is likewise; those that meditate and practice a spiritual path are also a minority.

With the body reminding us constantly that something should be done, we then need to realize that it is actually the reaction in the mind that brings about the suffering. Referring once more to the unpleasant feelings that arise when sitting in meditation, we need only see that if we have no reaction to them, we have no suffering. This is a very important practice point, which can be recognized here and now. We don't have to hope to get rid of pain in the future; we have the opportunity now. We learn without great difficulty that unpleasant feelings are only painful if we reject them and want them to be otherwise. If we accept things as they are, an unpleasant feeling is just a feeling, and no suffering arises.

That unsatisfactoriness stands at the apex of transcendental dependent arising is clear, because it also stands at the apex of the Buddha's explanation of his enlightenment. The very first thing he said was, "There is the noble truth of unsatisfactoriness." This is often misunderstood to mean that the Buddha's teaching is pessimistic, or that it stresses only the suffering, pain, and unhappiness that are inherent in us. But it is just the opposite. His teaching shows us realistically what is unsatisfactory and how to overcome it.

It is often thought that the Buddha's doctrine teaches us that suffering will disappear if one has meditated long enough, or if one sees everything differently. It is not that at all. Suffering isn't going to go away; the one who suffers is going to go away. That is the way of transcendental dependent arising.

The Buddha said, "There is the deed but no doer; there is suffering but no sufferer, there is the path but no one to enter, there is liberation but no one to attain it." If "I" want liberation, it is out of reach. The saying may sound like a Zen-inspired paradox, but it will become quite clear as we go along.

All of us experience the reality of the unsatisfactoriness of existence, since we are rarely totally satisfied with our life. We have all experienced occasions in the past that we would rather not have happened. There are others that we have wanted to come about but didn't. The best way to look at unsatisfactoriness is with gratitude, that it is happening in order to teach us some very important lesson. It is useless to want unsatisfactoriness to go away. It is impermanent, it will go away anyway, but if we don't learn the lesson that it is trying to teach us, it will come back in exactly the same manner. If we learn one particular lesson, unsatisfactoriness will return in a different form, until we see it for what it is, namely universal existence, nothing else. None of us has a monopoly on suffering. None of us is picked out to have a particular suffering. It just is.

The acceptance of "it just is" is the first step toward realizing this path. Unsatisfactoriness is. There are people who live very pleasant lives yet who can still realize it. There are others who live very unpleasant lives and don't realize it at all, but blame circumstances. They blame the government, or sometimes the atom bomb, or at other times the economy. People have all sorts of ideas about what can be blamed. Yet they could see in their own lives that there is a need to learn and grow. Every day we have an opportunity to learn, as there is hardly a human being without some daily suffering.

Pain need not necessarily be physical, although that aspect in particular helps us to see the connection between the first and second noble truth, so that one may actually practice within these guidelines. The connection is the wanting, the desire either to have or to eliminate. In all our experiences of unpleasantness, that is the underlying cause. Once we are aware of the cause, we can investigate what it is that compels us either to want this or not want that. We can learn to drop these responses, and this will help our lives to flow with far more ease, and will set much latent energy free for the practice of this path. While we are still using our mental capacities to want certain things and reject others, we are not free to use our energy to practice with great determination.

I once gave a meditation course to some young teenagers, and I wanted them to have a personal experience of getting rid of unsatisfactoriness. I asked them to undertake an experiment. They were to investigate whether anything in particular was making them feel dissatisfied or unhappy; then, for just one moment, they were to drop the wish of either having or not having, and find out whether unsatisfactoriness would disappear.

The next day I asked whether they had tried the experiment. One girl said she had, so I asked her to describe it. She said that since coming to the meditation course she had been coveting my little bell with its colorful cushion and tassel; in fact, she'd been pondering how to make one like that and where she could get the materials, or how she could find out where to purchase one. After I had told them about unsatisfactoriness, she realized that this thought process was making her very unhappy and agitated. So she determined to forget about bell, cushion, and tassel, and now she felt happy.

I might recommend the same kind of experiment to you. Of course, our material needs are well taken care of in the West, but we can still look inside ourselves and find out what makes us dissatisfied, or what has some kind of hold on us that gives us anxiety or worry. Is it the future? What particular aspect of it? For a moment, then, we can drop the whole of this thought process. When we let go, the relief becomes apparent. After having done this for one moment, maybe we can do the same again many times, for many moments. It is a worthwhile experiment, especially when we find something within that has repeatedly been giving us pain, a recurring pain agitator. It's always the experience that counts, not the concept.

We can compare this with the taste of the mango. If we try to tell somebody what a mango tastes like, all we can say is, "It tastes very nice; it's sweet and delicious, very juicy and soft." But does the person know what a mango tastes like? We have to bite into it, and only then do we know. It's not a peach, it's not an apricot, and it's a mango, different and distinctive. The same goes for everything taught by the Buddha: we must experience it ourselves. We have his guidelines, clear and uncompromising, which are of the utmost importance. When we use these instructions without injecting our own views, we can understand our experiences and thereby gain insight. That is why the words of the Buddha are of such importance to us—but only when we use them. To know them is the first step, to remember them the second, and the third is actually to work with that transmission in order to realize the truth for ourselves. These three steps encourage wisdom to arise.

QUESTIONS

STUDENT: *I would like to explore how the pain of existence becomes the path and no longer perpetuates itself. I know you've been talking about this, but I want to make sure that I understand it, because it is so easy to forget. For instance, when I feel bodily pain it is often easy to say, "This is just the body, which is impermanent, and I am getting older and will die." But when it comes to mental pain, I say to myself, "I really should practice, because this feels terrible." But then sometimes practice goes the wrong way. It just makes things worse. That's the point I want to explore further.*

AYYA KHEMA: Let me ask you this first: when you say "practice," do you mean you want to sit down and meditate?

S: *Yes.*

AK: Meditation is not all there is to practice. There's more than that.

S: *Whatever aspect you would like to enlarge on would be a help.*

AK: When there is mental pain, it would be very surprising if you could sit down and meditate. It would be unusual for the mind to be able to focus on a subject of meditation.

S: *Well, I attempt to sit down and meditate but I am really just sitting down experiencing pain.*

AK: That is correct. What you could do at such a time would be contemplation. Sit down where nobody will disturb you, and focus on the pain to find out its cause, why it should have arisen. Do not be satisfied with an answer such as "Because so-and-so said something"—that's only the superficial cause of it. That would have been the trigger, but there's no cause for mental pain unless there's something inside oneself that is reacting to that trigger. It is useful first to find the outer trigger, which is probably well known to you. It could be a sense of futility, anxiety about the future—any kind of trigger is possible. Then you need to find in yourself the reason for the reaction creating pain. The reason has to be "I don't want it the way it is." There can be no other. But why don't we like it the way it is? Usually the answer is "Because my ego is not supported." The bottom line of the whole inquiry is always "ego," but it's useless to say, "I know it is my ego" and then continue to have the pain. It is useful, however, to go through the whole process of the trigger, the personal reaction, the inquiry into the cause of the reaction, and then the understanding that the reaction is our suffering and not the trigger.

I have a formula: "Don't blame the trigger." Never let the mind stay with the trigger; always investigate what and who is reacting. Unless we find the reaction to the trigger in ourselves, we are going to repeat the same performance with the same result over and over again, like a preprogrammed computer printout. Press the same buttons and the same printout appears, until we finally realize that it is nothing but a button being pressed, and that we don't have to have the same printout. We are in a position to be able to stop ourselves. In the beginning that may be painful because we have to look at ourselves in a new way. We need not have this exaggerated idea of our own worth, nor do we need an exaggerated idea of our nonworth. We can learn just to accept the way things are. Sitting on the pillow at such a time is very good, but trying to meditate is often useless; contemplate instead. The subject of the contemplation is to be: "The cause of the mental pain."

S: *It is well explained that mental pain is a reaction, and I can understand the ego's defenses, but at that point it doesn't seem to be enough simply to con-*

sider that, because it does come up again. In fact, the next time it comes up, I have the extra irritation of knowing that it was going to happen again and that I won't be able to stop myself.

AK: Do you mean that after having gone through the whole inquiry, and having realized that it is just the ego reacting, you will react again? This is very natural. What we know and what we can do are miles apart. It will have to happen several times before you are able to say, "Let go, it doesn't matter." It takes time. We know so many things that we can't do yet, but knowing is our only hope of ever being able to act, otherwise we can't even begin. If we realize that it is only the ego wanting support and appreciation, we can eventually shed the compulsion to get recognition from outside sources. We are then able to go inside and find out whether there really is an ego, other than in our consciousness, and in our own perception. One day we will realize that there isn't anything. At that time, of course, there's no longer a need for support from outside.

Even while we are still working on this, we will find that our own inner support system will have grown through the meditative practice, and that we no longer have to search so constantly for outer support. One of the problems people often have in their lives is that they look for an emotional support system and are unable to find a suitable one. Our inner acceptance and reduced desires take care of that problem through enhanced meditation practice.

As we keep on practicing meditation, introspection, and contemplation, we are slowly, gently forming different views, and the flow of life changes. How quickly that will happen and how far the changes will reach is impossible to say. It depends on one's own determination and on having a state of mind unimpaired by too many viewpoints, which are very detrimental to one's progress.

S: *I believe you mentioned the aggregates. At what point in the aggregates[6] can we step out of the wheel of birth and death?*

AK: That explanation belongs to a further step along dependent arising. "Seeing things as they really are" is an insight arising out of practice. From a practical standpoint, when an unpleasant feeling arises, whether as a physical condition or as a mental state, we can realize that this is just a feeling, that it isn't "me" or "mine." We haven't asked it to come, it came by itself, so why do we think it belongs to "me"? Where does this consciousness of "me" and "mine" come into it? Eventually we realize that we are thinking of "me" and "mine" from habit, and that we can change that consciousness, but it naturally takes time and practice. Feeling, for instance, is a very strong aspect to work with.

Nobody likes to be sick, and yet the body does become sick. How then can there be this ownership of the body, if it does things it isn't supposed to do? If we really own something, we should be able to do what we like with it—throw it away, use it, give it away as a present, whatever we please—since it's ours. But what about this body? It does things we don't like and still we think we own it. These are very important contemplative aspects that we can use in the meditative procedure. For instance, in meditation we can look at one aspect of the aggregates, or several of them, and observe when and how they arise and cease. We can feel the body in the sitting position, and it may be generating unpleasant feelings; then we can inquire, "Is that mine? Does it belong to me? Is it really me? Why am I saying it's me? Where am I getting this idea from?" This is one way of working with the aggregates. The aggregates are the linchpin of ego delusion because all of our ego concept revolves around those five.

Another thing we can do is to investigate whether there's anything else to be found within ourselves other than the five aggregates. Once we are sure there is nothing else, we can ask, "Where is this 'me' that proclaims that all this is mine?" These are contemplations and can be done as a meditation. Does that answer the question?

S: *Yes. What really caught my interest was when you said that we could step out of the twelve steps of causation at the point between feeling and craving. I wondered whether it wouldn't be simpler if I could just find that little spot in the aggregates and do the same thing, since there are only five aggregates and there are twelve steps of causation.*

AK: Yes, of course. The other eleven steps are automatic results of causes. There is nothing we can do about them. Once the ignorance is there, the ego delusion has only one doorway out, namely, between feeling and craving.

As far as the five aggregates are concerned feeling is the one we live by. Therefore working with our feelings can be our most important growth process. When we get an unpleasant feeling, we learn to see that it doesn't belong to us, and therefore we don't have to react. But not because of indifference or suppression. That also presents a danger, since we can suppress feelings quite easily by putting our mind to something else. That would mean we are not acknowledging our feelings. Equanimity can only arise through accepting feelings with nonreaction, when we realize that although there is a feeling, it isn't "mine."

That point of departure, between feeling and craving, is exactly what we need to practice. We want the painful feelings to go away, but if they simply arise and we can let go again, then there is no hurt, no unsatisfactoriness. There are many approaches to lead us out of delusion where the ego can be seen for what it is—an impostor, public enemy number one.

S: *On the same subject: I am wondering how* vipassanā *helps in this process of separating the reaction from the feeling. You've mentioned contemplation.*

AK: You are asking about methods, are you? Feelings and reactions constantly come up in our daily lives, so the practice of mindfulness is necessary. The word *vipassanā* means insight, clear-seeing. It doesn't actually denote any particular method. It's the goal and the purpose of the whole practice path, and one of the two ways of using the meditative procedure, but the word doesn't denote any particular approach.

Insight can arise from introspection or contemplation, but not necessarily, and not for everyone. The Buddha compared Dhamma to a snake. He said if you pick a snake up by the tail, it will undoubtedly bite you; you have to pick it up behind the head to be safe. We have to pick up the Dhamma in the correct way, so that it doesn't hurt us. Introspection, which means mindfulness and attention to one's own inner world, can bring us an understanding of what a human being is.

So far I have only mentioned mindfulness of the body. The second step is mindfulness of feeling (*vedanânupassanā*), and I will teach you a method for that. Of course the method itself cannot suffice to bring wisdom, just as loving-kindness meditation is not sufficient to guarantee lovingness in our hearts. Methods are very helpful on our path, but internal mindfulness is essential—attention to oneself, to one's own reactions, to feelings both physical and emotional; a realization that the ego is the actor, and lastly, an inquiry as to whether that is necessary or not. It involves being attentive the whole day long. Contemplating the five aggregates as not "me," or the body as impermanent, are steps on the way, but the most important aspect is mindfulness in daily living.

S: *It seems that we all have perceptions, and then we have the reactions. Would the reactions be the ego part? There's no way we can get rid of perceptions. I am not sure whether feeling is actually part of that perception or whether it is part of the reaction.*

AK: Neither. It works like this. First there is the sense contact, and from the sense contact arises a feeling. After the feeling comes perception, and perception brings about the mental formation, which is the reaction. When we sit with our legs crossed, we first have the touch contact of sitting; following that an unpleasant feeling may develop; then perception, which says, "This is pain"; and then the reaction: "I don't like it, my blood circulation is going to stop; I am sure this is not necessary; I should have sat on a chair"—or whatever thoughts the mind may produce. We run the whole gamut of reaction. Between thinking "This is painful" and "I want to get rid of it" is the point of departure. Does this explain it? It is important to watch just this in the sitting position in meditation because here we have a good opportunity to experience our reactions.

S: *I think we are saying the same thing. Mindfulness would get you in touch with the pain and what is actually happening, and then, because you are mindful, you're right there with it, and you don't have to take the next step of wanting to leave.*

AK: Yes. Mindfulness acts like a brake on a car. If we drive a car without brakes, it's potential suicide. If we have brakes on a car, when coming to a dangerous corner we step on those brakes; slow the car down to the point where we can turn the steering wheel in a different direction and escape the danger. With mindfulness we experience exactly the same thing. When we step on the brake of mindfulness, we slow down and take time to consider what's happening. We don't have to say, "I can't stand you, I am leaving." We just slow down, realize that this is a dangerous corner, and change our direction. Mindfulness slows us down to the point where we can look inside and see ourselves clearly. That doesn't mean that we are able to handle all situations yet. The Buddha often advised his followers to associate with wise people, those who help one on this path. He mentioned this fact many times; we can infer, therefore, that it is natural not to be immune to some difficult situations, but at least we do not react impulsively and instinctively, which usually causes grief for both sides.

S: *I am interested in the notion of birth and what it is that's born from the viewpoint of enlightenment. What can be said about birth?*

AK: I think that the two traditions of Theravāda and Mahāyāna differ here. I can only answer you from the Theravāda tradition, to which I belong. In transcendental dependent arising we find ignorance (*avijja*), followed by karma, or mental formations (*sankhāra*), resulting in rebirth consciousness (*viññāna*). Rebirth consciousness is due to the "craving to be." The craving incorporates karmic residue found in that particular mind. What we are seeing as a rebirth, or as a birth, is the "craving to be here" joined with karmic residue and karmic resultants. We cannot say from an absolute standpoint that a person is being reborn; it just appears like that. From the relative standpoint, an individual is born. From the absolute standpoint, nothing is reborn except the karmic residue. I think in the Mahāyāna tradition there seems to be an idea of voluntary rebirth. The Theravāda tradition does not speak of that.

S: *The karmic formations cause birth; through meditation we would discover the insubstantial quality of mind and body, so that actually not having to be reborn would be simply discovering that nothing was ever born. Something like that?*

AK: Not quite. We are born. What we discover through this process of insight is that there is nothing worthwhile to be here for, and when we are able to go beyond existence, nothing is born, and so nothing dies. The person who is now here, who has been born, discovers that this "craving to be" here is totally unnecessary. In fact, it is an aberration of the mind, a fatal mistake, which always ends in a fatality.

LOVING-KINDNESS MEDITATION

Before starting, concentrate on the breath for just a moment.

Now think of yourself as your own best friend, and extend to yourself the care and concern, the love and attention, that you would give a best friend. Embrace yourself as your own best friend.

Think of the person sitting nearest you. Be that person's best friend, extending your love and compassion, your care, and concern, to him or her.

Think of yourself as the best friend of everyone who is present, and extend your love and compassion, friendship, care, and concern to everyone with you. Fill everyone and embrace everyone with your friendship.

Now think of yourself as your parents' best friend. Fill them with your love and concern, and embrace them with your friendship, letting them know how much you care.

Think of your nearest and dearest people, and be their best friend. Fill them with your care, your concern, and your love, embracing them with your friendship.

Now think of all your good friends. Let them feel that you are their best friend. Fill them with love, embrace them in friendship.

Think of anyone whom you find difficult to get along with or hard to love. Become that person's best friend, thereby removing all obstacles in your own heart. Embrace him or her with love and compassion.

Open your heart as wide as you can to as many people as possible, near and far. Let the feeling of care and concern, of love and compassion, reach out into the distance to as many beings as you can imagine, embracing them all in friendship.

Bring your attention back to yourself. Feel the happiness that comes from being your own best friend. The ease and harmony that you can feel comes from accepting yourself, caring for yourself, enjoying your own company, just like a best friend would.

May all beings be friends with each other.

⤙6 Faith and Confidence

Step 2

THE SECOND STEP in transcendental dependent arising is faith and confidence. When we have actually realized that unsatisfactoriness is inherent in worldly existence, there comes a time when we look for something not of a worldly nature that may relieve us of our unsatisfactoriness. If we find a spiritual teaching, faith or confidence in it may arise. Such confidence is a matter of the heart and not of the mind, because at the start of our practice we cannot possibly have our own experience of the teaching. Therefore, we cannot confirm that it is true, based on reasoning and knowledge. But a feeling in the heart can tell us that here is a transcendental truth, more profound than anything we have previously heard or read. Confidence and faith also contain love, since we can only be confident about something we love. If there is no heart connection, we can't trust implicitly.

Those who have much doubt find it very difficult to give themselves completely to anything or anyone. They always want to hold themselves back a bit, wishing to own part of themselves completely. As a result, they cannot flow wholeheartedly. If we hold ourselves back, our spiritual progress is very much impaired.

There is no closer relationship than the one we have with our own spiritual path. It is the closest connection we can possibly have. If we have a relationship with another person, such as in a marriage, and we don't give ourselves to it wholeheartedly, but have constant doubts about whether this is the right person and the right situation, the marriage will not be successful. Yet when one first gets married, one doesn't know what may eventuate. This also holds true for the spiritual path. When we first enter it, we don't know what may result. We don't understand a lot of the teaching yet. We have few reference points, because so far we haven't looked into ourselves deeply enough. However, unless we give ourselves to the path wholeheartedly, our practice cannot possibly be a success.

Few people are capable of wholehearted commitment, and that is why so few people experience a real transformation through their spiritual practice. It is a matter of giving up our own viewpoints, of letting go of opinions and preconceived ideas, and of following the Buddha's guidelines instead. Although this sounds simple, in practice most people find it extremely difficult. Their ingrained viewpoints, based on deductions derived from cultural and social norms, are in the way.

We must also remember that heart and mind need to work together. If we understand something rationally but don't love it, there is no completeness for us, no fulfillment. If we love something but don't understand it, the same applies. If we have a relationship with another person, and we love the person but don't understand him or her, the relationship is incomplete; if we understand the person but don't love him or her, it is equally unfulfilling. How much more so on our spiritual path. We have to understand the meaning of the teaching, and also love it. In the beginning our understanding will only be partial, so our love has to be even greater.

Faith and confidence are based on the opening of the heart, and the letting go of our own notions of what the teaching and the teacher should represent. Our expectations need to be discarded, since they are based on assumptions and not facts. We can become like a child holding his mother's hand to cross a busy street, having confidence that his mother will know best. If we are able to give ourselves in that way, a feeling of happiness arises.

The Buddha compared faith to a blind giant who meets up with a very sharp-eyed cripple, called Wisdom. The blind giant, called Faith, says to the sharp-eyed cripple, "I am very strong, but I can't see; you are very weak, but you have sharp eyes. Come and ride on my shoulders. Together we will go far." The Buddha never supported blind faith, but a balance between heart and mind, between wisdom and faith. The two together will go far.

The saying that blind faith can move mountains unfortunately omits the fact that, being blind, faith doesn't know which mountain needs moving. That's where wisdom is essential, which means that a thorough understanding of the teaching is crucial. Even if, at the beginning, the Dhamma seems difficult or alien, we have to make our inquiry wholeheartedly. If we work on anything, whether planting a garden or building a house, it has to be done wholeheartedly. That kind of endeavor promises success. Everything else is like dabbling in yet another new hobby.

Only when we have realized that there is no other way out of unsatisfactoriness will we be ready to immerse ourselves deeply. If we are still looking for a loophole, looking for happiness in the world, our commitment to the spiritual practice is not complete. Spiritual practice touches upon the raw edges in ourselves and reaches deeply within, where in the end we may not recognize ourselves any more. We can compare this to turning ourselves inside out; that which we like to hide from ourselves and others has to be made visible. Only then can it be healed. Because this is difficult and often painful, our commitment has to be total, deriving from the understanding of understanding.

If we think the world has the answer to our quest for happiness, only we haven't found it yet, we surely will not engage in such a difficult task, but rather we will continue looking for the missing link in the world. The world is so full of manifold distractions and manifold opportunities, temptations, and beauty that a whole lifetime is not sufficient to explore it all.

We need total conviction, not only of unsatisfactoriness, but also of truth when we hear it, with our mind being fully attuned. The Buddha said that "those who have little dust in their eyes" when hearing the truth will know it to be the truth, and wholehearted commitment follows. This doesn't mean that we can no longer fulfill our daily obligations. On the contrary, we can attend to them much better, because they are now just a side issue, no longer the main item. Priority is given to our spiritual growth.

Our daily activities, while still taking up time, energy, and responsibility, no longer seem to impinge on us in the same manner that they used to when they were our only concern. We looked for perfection in these activities, because otherwise we would have felt we were lacking ability. Now we can see their changing and repetitive nature, necessary to keep alive, but resembling the revolutions of a merry-go-round. No longer are they the only important aspect of our lives, and this results in more ease of living. We are not so concerned about being correct or perfect, because we know there is something more profound that matters far more to us.

From this point onward we watch over our spiritual growth as we would over a fragile plant in our garden. We nurture, feed, and protect it from all adversity. Our whole human existence is fragile as long as we have not yet become one of the noble ones; only then will we be secure. Until such a time, there is always the danger of making bad karma, of indulgence, and of anger that may retard our growth.

We could become quite satisfied with ourselves because we are sitting in meditation and are endeavoring to practice the spiritual path. Such satisfaction with ourselves is not the same as contentment. Contentment is necessary, self-satisfaction is detrimental. To be content has to include knowing we are in the right place at the right time to facilitate our own growth. But to be self-satisfied means that we no longer realize the need for growth. All these aspects are important parts of our commitment, and they make us into one whole being with a one-pointed direction.

Confidence is indispensable on the spiritual path. Of the Three Jewels—the Buddha, Dhamma, and Sangha—the Dhamma is the most important for us.

At the time of the Buddha there was a monk who was so infatuated with the Buddha that he followed him around like a puppy dog. Wherever the Buddha went, this monk went too. One day the monk became very ill and had to stay in bed. As he was lying in bed he started crying. When the other monks came to see him, they asked him, "Why are you crying? You are not that ill. What's the matter?"

He said, "I am crying because, being ill, I can't see the Buddha."

The other monks replied, "Do not worry, we'll tell the Buddha. He will come and visit you."

Upon learning this, the Buddha immediately came to visit the sick monk, who brightened up and looked happy again. Then the Buddha said to him, "Whoever sees me sees the Dhamma; whoever sees the Dhamma sees me."

Whoever sees a buddha sees nothing but enlightenment, which is the essence of the Dhamma. Whoever can see the Dhamma within sees the Buddha, equaling enlightenment. The greatest jewel is recognizing the Dhamma in oneself and not being attached to any one person, even the Buddha, who only wants to be our guide. When true confidence arises in the Dhamma, it gives great impetus to the practice. Such a jewel is worth more than any precious thing in the whole world, because it enables us to surpass and transcend all worldly problems and difficulties. They do not disappear, but we no longer recognize them as a hindrance because we have seen absolute truth.

Faith and confidence as an indispensable part of spiritual practice include reverence and gratitude. These are qualities that we can deliberately foster in ourselves, as they are not so commonly expressed. We need some ideal to revere, and we can be grateful that we have now found one worth honoring, namely the greatest jewel that exists, the law of nature, the Dhamma, which shows us absolute reality. Reverence for that is embodied in our attitude to life around us, because there is nothing in the whole of existence that does not contain the Dhamma, which itself is impermanence, unsatisfactoriness, and corelessness. Wherever we look, outside or inside, everything proclaims that Dhamma. Reverence for Dhamma enables us to have compassion for life and for all that exists, because there is nothing but these three characteristics, and therefore everything contains suffering. Our love and respect for the Dhamma is recognizable in our attitude toward others and toward our practice. In the Japanese Zen tradition we find a very nice custom of meditators greeting their cushion and other meditators before they sit down, showing reverence for the cushion they are going to use and the persons practicing with them.

The more we can imbue ourselves with such attitudes, the more gentle and accepting we will feel. Reverence shows that there is something greater than we are ourselves, greater than our own opinions and abilities, something we can use as an ultimate goal. Reverence is a commitment to faith.

Gratitude is an expression of love and connectedness and it may be extended toward the teaching, the practice, the place, the other practitioners, toward everyone and everything that forms part of life. We can be grateful for our good karma enabling us to enter the Noble Path. All these qualities—faith, confidence, and gratitude—help us to empty ourselves of personal pride and some of our personality beliefs, because we have found a greater reality beyond our limited self-concern.

Faith, which is inspired by the truth we hear, needs a firm foundation of inquiry and love, but it should never be blind. The Buddha said, "The whole of the universe, oh monks, lies in this fathom-long body and mind." (The fathom is an old-fashioned measurement, which today might be translated as six feet or so.) If the whole universe can be found in our own body and mind, this is where we need to make our inquiries. We all have the answers within ourselves, we just have not gotten in touch with them yet. The potential of finding the truth within requires faith in ourselves. Without it, we will often waver and will not be able to succeed to the very end. Complete and utter faith means that we are sure of the path, although we haven't experienced the truth yet. It is an inner agreement, an inner acceptance, and a turning wholly toward transcendence in order to provide relief, release, freedom, liberation.

If the whole universe lies in our body and mind, we also need love for ourselves. If we can't love, we can't have faith. We need the love that embraces commitment, a feeling of wholeness within ourselves and with the practice, of not being split into two, sometimes practicing and at other times forgetting. When there is faith and confidence, the result is a totality of being and direction.

QUESTIONS

STUDENT: *If there is corelessness, whom do we love? Isn't that a contradiction?*

AYYA KHEMA: It only seems like a contradiction because there are two levels of understanding. On the level of absolute truth there isn't anything. No birth, no death, no person. But on the level of relative truth, we have to work with our emotions and our difficulties. We're talking on a relative level, because on the absolute level we wouldn't be speaking to each other. There would be nobody there for discussion. On our level, love is the important emotion. Sometimes this may sound like a paradox, but we can only work on the relative level. Once we have reached the absolute level, we have nothing to say.

S: *I am starting to accumulate questions. I have two at this point. Does contemplation lead to insight for everyone? Also, you said earlier that one cannot meditate when unhappy or without joy. Could you please explain?*

AK: Contemplation should lead to insight, but that is the same as saying that meditation should lead to liberation. Not everybody has enough determination and perseverance to gain insight. If we contemplate a universal truth such as impermanence, our mind may balk at deeper levels of understanding and refuse to reach a point where it becomes meaningful. The mind may say, "All is impermanent, certainly," and then give up. Insight only arises when impermanence is seen as such a penetrating aspect of ourselves that nothing solid can be found. It's quite possible that one contemplates and yet one still fails to gain any insight.

S: *What is the cause of that, and what can be done about it?*

AK: It is caused by fear, which is a human condition…the fear of annihilation of this supposed person, either through physical death or not enough emotional ego support, and it may arise particularly when we come near to seeing impermanence in ourselves very strongly. Then there is great fear, even panic, that we may find a truth we don't want to know, namely that this identity, this personality, is a myth. Fear is the first and foremost hindrance to going deeper. When the meditation improves, all these fears disappear, because meditation itself becomes a substitute for our own viewpoints. In the beginning, fear is the greatest obstacle. The remedy is perseverance.

S: *Why do you say that one cannot meditate when unhappy or without joy?*

AK: One can certainly try to meditate, but the result will be unsatisfactory. The mind that is unhappy and bothered by something will constantly return to that bother—as when you have an itch and constantly return to scratch that same itch. The mind has to be at ease, at peace, in order to become really calm. So far, we have used a method for meditation which is equivalent to a training period. Soon we will discuss how it becomes true meditation. The mind has to be calm and at ease in order to become absorbed.

S: *Is it true that as long as there is some kind of discursiveness—in other words, as long as this problem or that problem keeps intervening—we don't have true meditation? And if this is so, should we persist?*

AK: Absolutely.

S: *You mentioned that the spiritual path may turn one inside out. One's problems, which one would rather not expose, are exposed. Yet one should have calm and peace. So how does that contradiction resolve itself? Anyone who has practiced knows that a lot of things come up that don't help one to be calm.*

AK: That is quite true. We resist, are ashamed, and blame ourselves for our difficulties and defilements, and would much rather they hadn't arisen. That introduces turbulence into the mind and is detrimental to meditation. However, if we accept all that we see in ourselves, then abandon it and substitute wholesome thinking, no agitation will follow. If we accept things the way they are, and do not try to alter them, and if we keep impermanence and nonself in mind, we shall gain the needed learning experience without emotional turmoil. Even though one hasn't realized corelessness yet, if we have faith in the Buddha's teaching, we know it is the ultimate truth. In that case, there is nothing to worry about when we turn ourselves inside out and some of the rubbish shows. We are keeping the whole of the teaching in mind, and specifically that which brings liberation. Then we learn to be grateful for the defilements; if we deal with them in a sensible manner, we may be able to let go and avoid falling into the same errors again. Naturally, there will be times when we can't just drop our habitual responses and the defilements will recur. It would be nice if this didn't happen, but if we understand this and just accept it, it's no tragedy. On the contrary, it is just another of our lessons on this path.

S: *I find it very difficult to combine the ordinary day-to-day life in New York, where I live, with spiritual practice. Do you have any suggestions?*

AK: It is quite true, of course, that there will be difficulties. Eventually, we find our own priorities. If it is more important to follow the spiritual path and make that our life, we will find our way out of Manhattan, maybe to Pleasant Bay. There are always some people who are able to do it, because they have seen a different reality. But if we are caught up in the distractions and temptations of ordinary life, we won't see clearly enough to find out just yet. Maybe at a later stage...

S: *This is probably going to sound like a very vague question. I really seem to be confused. You seem to stress that whatever comes up isn't workable. You are not really saying that, are you?*

AK: No. Please continue with your question.

S: *I studied on my own many of Chögyam Trungpa Rinpoche's books, and some of this seems to me to contradict his teaching. I always had the impression that whatever came up is really valuable, only distorted; that we can take whatever comes up and really get into it and work with it. It seems to me that you are saying that although we have to work with it, though perhaps to a lesser degree, we should then get rid of it and go for this ideal.*

AK: When you say "whatever comes up," are you talking about thoughts? Or something else?

S: *Strong emotions. Overwhelming emotions.*

AK: Emotions and thoughts during meditation, is that what you are asking about? A very important way to work with these is to label them, drop them, and then go back to the breath. To get into them and explore them would halt any meditative procedure. That couldn't even be called contemplation, because these are personal and not universal emotions. When we can change the individual problem into a universal application, it could be used for contemplation.

You are actually looking at different stages of development in meditation. Meditation develops slowly for most people. In the beginning we try to keep the subject of meditation in mind—in this case the breath—and label whatever arises in order to gain insight into ourselves. We give the disturbance a name, identify it, so that we know what it is; then we drop it and get back to the breath. The thought or emotion dissolves by itself after having been labeled, because we have become an objective observer. We are no longer subjective. As an observer we watch the occurrence, but we do not go into it, and therefore there is space for the emotion to fold up and vanish. These are very important lessons which all of us need to learn.

As one continues, meditation becomes more one-pointed so that one can begin to experience absorption. Meditation absorptions are the means, not the goal, of meditation; however, they are a necessary means for gaining insight. The mind that has problems is concerned with solving or lamenting them but is not geared to insight into absolute reality, which is the goal of meditation. We need to prepare the mind to become so calm, one-pointed, and strong that it will no longer flinch when it is confronted by the deepest truth. People who have been meditating for some years do not usually experience as many defilements and distractions as they did at the beginning.

S: *Well, absorption might have thrown me off. I don't really relate to that very well.*

AK: The word?

S: *The state.*

AK: Not having experienced it is comparable to not having tasted a mango. It's difficult to talk about the taste of a mango when one doesn't know what it is. But at least we can be aware that such meditative states exist and are part of transcendental dependent arising. Does that sound better? "Meditative absorption" is the English translation of the Pali word *jhāna*, which is much shorter and much more to the point.

❧|7 Mindfulness of Feelings and Sensations: A Technique of Meditation

I WILL EXPLAIN THE PURPOSE, usefulness, aim, and direction of this meditation method after we have gone through it together. Without the experience, we cannot become fully involved. At this time we need to familiarize ourselves with a spot in the body that we call the "top of the head," which is a shallow indentation that we all have on the top of our skulls. In a baby it is the fontanel, where the bones grow together later. We can find it three or four fingers' width above the hairline. The other spot is the crown of the head, which is about the size of a large coin, where the hair grows in a different direction. Some people have it on the left, others on the right, some in the middle. It doesn't matter where we find it; it simply gives a location.

Start by paying attention to the feeling that is generated by the wind of the breath at the nostrils. Become aware of that feeling for a few moments.

Now transfer your attention to the "top of the head." Let everything else go; pay no more attention to the breath. Just put your full awareness on the top of the head and notice any feeling that is to be found there: ticklishness, heaviness, pressure, tingling, contraction, expansion, warmth, cold, pleasantness, unpleasantness, movement, stillness—any of those, or any others. You don't need to name the sensation, although you can if you wish. I am only naming them in order to help.

Slowly move your attention from the top of the head to the crown of the head, along the top of the skull, spot after spot, becoming aware of each spot. Note the sensation, the feeling; let go and move on to the next spot.

Try to cover the whole of the top of the skull. Sensation is physical; feeling is emotional. Note anything that may arise; let go, and focus on the next spot: hardness, softness, pressure, tingling, tickling, movement, contraction, expansion, warmth, poking, stabbing, disliking...the sensation may be on the skin or under the skin. It may be deep inside or on the surface. The only thing that really matters is awareness.

Now concentrate on the crown of the head, a small area. Become aware of how it feels. Try to get so close to yourself that feelings and sensations become apparent.

Slowly move your attention from the crown of the head along the back of the skull to the base, where the neck joins the head. Pay full attention to each spot, noting, letting go, going on to the next one.

Now place your full attention on the left side of the head, slowly moving down from the top of the skull to the jaw line, from the hairline in front to behind the left ear. Concentrate on each spot, slowly moving down, becoming aware of either feeling or sensation...noting solidity, touch, tension, relaxation, resistance, anything that arises. Note it, let it go, and move on to the next spot.

Bring your attention to the right side of the head, slowly moving down from the top of the skull to the jaw line, from the hairline in front to behind the right ear. Pay full attention to each spot as you slowly move down, knowing the sensation, knowing the feeling, on the skin or under the skin, deep inside or on the surface. It's the awareness that counts.

Put your full attention on the hairline above the forehead and slowly move down the whole width of the forehead to the eyebrows, spot by spot. Note whatever may present itself: pounding, movement, pressure, pleasantness, unpleasantness.

Now turn your full attention to the left eye, all around it—socket, eyeball, lid—and notice the sensation, the feeling: pressure, heaviness, darkness, light, touch, trembling, stillness.

Next transfer your attention to your right eye. All around—socket, eyeball, lid. Take note of any sensation, any feeling that you become aware of.

Concentrate on the spot between the eyebrows. Slowly move down the nose to the tip, noticing spot after spot: hardness, softness, tingling—it can be any of these, or any other sensation that you are aware of.

Now fix your attention on the nostrils. Slowly move up inside the nose, noticing the sensation: air, movement, space, confinement, openness, ticklishness, wetness, dryness, touch.

Concentrate on the small area between the tip of the nose and the upper lip, the width of the upper lip. Notice any sensation, any feeling: touch, movement, trembling, stillness, heaviness, lightness.

Move your attention to the upper and lower lip. Notice touch, pressure, contraction, wetness, dryness, pleasantness, unpleasantness, any of these or any others.

Place your attention on the inside of the mouth. Become aware of any sensation, any feeling. Move from spot to spot, covering the whole area.

Put your full attention on the chin. Become aware of what it feels like.

Move your attention to the left cheek, slowly moving down from the eye to the jaw line. With your attention on each spot, notice any sensation, any feeling; let go and move to the next spot.

Concentrate on the right cheek, slowly moving down from the eye to the jaw line, spot by spot. Become aware of sensation or feeling; noticing, letting go, and moving on to the next spot. The sensation can be faint or definite, it doesn't matter.

Put your attention on the throat. Slowly move down from the jaw line to where the neck joins the trunk, spot by spot, outside or inside, noticing touch, warmth, obstruction, heaviness, lightness, pulsing.

Move your attention to the back of the neck, starting at the base of the skull and slowly moving down to where the neck joins the trunk. Notice each spot: tense, relaxed, knotted, pleasant, unpleasant, poking, stabbing, tickling, tingling—any of these, or any others.

Put your full attention on the left shoulder. Slowly move from the neck along the top of the shoulder to where the left arm joins. Notice each spot, becoming aware of the feeling or sensation: tense, relaxed, heavy, burdened, whatever it may be, noticing it, letting go, and moving on to the next spot.

Now turn your attention to the left upper arm, slowly moving down from the shoulder to the elbow, all around the left upper arm, becoming aware of each spot as you move along. Notice the sensation, the feeling; let go and then go on to the next spot. Notice touch, warmth, movement, heaviness, lightness, contraction, expansion.

Concentrate on the left elbow. It is a small area, so let everything else go. Pay no attention to any other part of the body, only the left elbow, and notice the feeling, the sensation.

Put your full attention on the left lower arm. Slowly moving down from the elbow to the wrist, all around, spot by spot; notice, let go, and move on to the next spot, on the skin or under the skin, surface or deep inside. Come close to your own feelings, to your own sensations.

Move your attention to the left wrist, all around. Notice pulsing, pounding, contracting, touching.

Next concentrate on the back of the left hand, from the wrist to where the fingers join. Put your attention on the palm of the left hand, from the wrist to where the fingers join. Focus your attention on the bottom of the five fingers of the left hand. Slowly move along the fingers to their tips. Have your full attention on the five tips and then make a mind movement outward, from the tips out into the room.

Put your full attention on the right shoulder. Slowly moving from the neck along the top of the shoulder to where the right arm joins. Notice each spot: heavy, contracted, knotted, tense, relaxed, burdened, painful, grief, anger, resistance, anything at all. Notice it, let go, and move on to the next spot.

Move your attention to the right upper arm. Slowly move down from the shoulder to the elbow, all around the right upper arm. Spot after spot, on the skin or under the skin: hardness, softness, warmth, cold, touch, movement, stillness.

Concentrate on the right elbow. Let everything else go; pay attention only to that small area, and notice what it feels like: tingly, contracted, electric.

Place your attention on the right lower arm. Slowly move down from the elbow to the wrist, all around: soft, hard, pleasant, tingling.

Put your full attention on the right wrist, all around. Notice the surface or deep inside.

Next move your attention to the back of the right hand, from the wrist to where the fingers join. Put your attention on the palm of the right hand, from the wrist to where the fingers join. Focus your full attention on the bottom of the five fingers of the right hand. Slowly move along the fingers to the tips. Keep your full attention on the five tips and make a mind movement outward, from the tips into the room.

Put your full attention on the left side of the front of the trunk.

Slowly move down from the left shoulder to the waist, touching upon each spot as you move your attention. Notice feeling or sensation: restriction, expansion, stabbing, poking, heaviness, lightness, tingling, hardness, softness, rejection, resistance, worry, fear; whatever comes to the surface, notice, let go, and move to the next spot.

Move your attention to the right side of the front of the trunk, slowly moving down from the right shoulder to the waist, touching upon each spot with full awareness.

Put your full attention on the waistline in front. Notice the sensation: tightness, looseness. Slowly move from the waist to the groin, down the lower part of the trunk, spot after spot, being aware of sensation, feeling, letting go, and moving to the next spot, becoming aware of what each spot feels like.

Put your attention on the left side of the back, slowly moving down from the shoulder to the waist, paying attention to each spot, becoming aware of the sensation and feeling, letting go and noticing the next spot: tension, knottiness, worry, heaviness, touch, warmth, movement, hardness, softness, tingling.

Put your full attention on the right side of the back, slowly moving down from the shoulder to the waist, with full awareness on each spot.

Put your full attention on the waistline at the back: contracted, expanded, cramped, poking, stabbing. Starting at the waistline, slowly move down to the left buttock as far as where the leg joins. Notice spot after spot, on the skin, under the skin, deep inside, or on the surface; be aware of sensation or feeling. Notice, let go, move to the next spot: heaviness, touch, pressure.

Move to the right side of the waist at the back. Slowly shift your attention down to the right buttock, to where the right leg joins. Notice each spot, each sensation.

Concentrate on the right thigh. Slowly move down from the groin to the knee, all around, noticing pressure, touch, unpleasantness, stabbing, poking. Notice, drop it, and go on to the next spot.

Concentrate on the right knee, all around, outside, inside.

Place your attention on the right lower leg. Slowly move down from the knee to the ankle, all around, getting to know each spot.

Put your attention on the right ankle. Notice pressure, touch, hardness, softness.

Have your full attention on the right heel, a small area. Let everything else go, just be there.

Put your full attention on the sole of the right foot, from the heel to where the toes join. Be aware of each spot. Notice sensation or feeling: smoothness, roughness, warmth, touch, stabbing, pulling.

Put your attention on the top of the right foot, from the ankle to where the toes join, spot by spot, noticing inside or outside. Put your full attention on the base of the five toes of the right foot. Slowly move along the toes to their tips. Put your full attention on the five tips and make a mind movement outward, from the tips into the room.

Next move your attention to the left thigh. Slowly move down from the groin to the knee, all around the left thigh, spot by spot. Notice, let go, and move to the next spot.

Put your full attention on the left knee, all around, inside, outside, fully aware of feelings and sensations.

Concentrate on the left lower leg. Slowly move down from the knee to the ankle, all around. Notice pressure, heaviness, solidity, hardness, touch, poking, stabbing, tingling. Whatever it may be, notice it, drop it, and move to the next spot.

Put your full attention on the left ankle, all around. Notice touch, pressure, resistance, rejection.

Move your attention to the left heel, a small area. Let everything else go. Be only there.

Put your full attention on the sole of the left foot. Slowly move from the heel to where the toes join. Notice each spot: pressure, touch, warmth.

Put your full attention on the top of the left foot, from the ankle to where the toes join, spot by spot, noticing, being fully aware. Move your attention to the base of the five toes of the left foot. Slowly move along the toes to their tips. Put your full attention on the five tips. Make a mind movement outward, from the tips into the room.

This method of meditation is often called *vipassanā*, but that is actually a misnomer, because *vipassanā* means "insight." A method cannot claim insight; insight develops from clarity of mind. Therefore, we commonly call it "sweeping," though we mustn't think of a broom in this connection. The "sweeping" we have just done is called "part by part."

In one aspect, this is a method of purification. Because the whole of the Buddha's path is one of purification, anything we can use to help us along is a welcome aid. This method of purification is quite specific, as becomes clear when we remember that our physical reactions to our emotions are constant and immediate, and we are unable ever to stop them. If we are happy, which is an emotion, we are likely to smile or laugh. If we are unhappy, we are likely to cry, to make an unhappy face, or to frown. If we are angry, we may become red in the face or rigid. If we feel anxiety, maybe in heavy city traffic, our shoulders contract; there are very few people who do not have tension in their shoulders. It is immaterial which emotion is linked to a particular part of the body.

Our emotional reactions have no other way of manifesting themselves than through our body. Since birth, we have been dealing with our emotions in this manner, or maybe we could say "misdealing." The body has always reacted and has eventually retained some of these reactions in the form of tensions and blockages. This meditation method has the potential for removing blockages, or at least rendering them somewhat less obstructive, depending on the strength of our concentration, and also on our karma.

Imagine for a moment that some people have been living in this room for the past thirty years, and have never cleaned it up. They have left remains of food, excrement, dirty clothes, and dirty dishes, and have never swept the floor. By now the place is dirty and messy from floor to ceiling. Then a friend comes along and says to the occupants, "Why don't you sweep at least a little corner where you can sit down comfortably?" Our friends who are living here do that and find that the clean little corner is far more comfortable than their previous situation, although they couldn't have imagined that before cleaning it up. Now they are motivated to clean up the whole place. They find that they can now see out of the windows, and the whole prospect of living in this place has become much more pleasant. Of course, a person living here could have moved somewhere else when the mess became too unmanageable, but we are all stuck with our body. We can't move away from it. We can change our living quarters many times in one lifetime—from the city to the country, from an apartment to a house, from being with friends to being alone, from one country to another—but our body always accompanies us. It is our permanent abode until it breaks up and dies, and crumbles to dust. While we still have our body we may as well try to do our best with it, because otherwise it is a bother and a disruption in our meditation. It does all sorts of things we don't want it to do.

When we take a shower or a bath, all we can do is to wash our skin. We all know that we consist of more than just skin, yet that is all that we ever clean. Day after day, we have nice, clean skin and probably clean hair too. That's about all we accomplish. The *vipassanā* method in its first application can be likened to an internal shower. What the mind has put in through emotional reactions, the mind can remove by letting go.

Letting go is the open secret of purification. Every time we move from one place in the body to the next, we have let go of whatever arose in the previous spot. In the end we let go through our fingertips and our toes out into the room, because there is no longer any other body part to which we can move. We are thereby cleaning up, taking an internal shower, removing some of the inner blockages. Since this is a great help physically, our minds also feel more at ease. We don't have as many difficulties with the body any more, and we can use our mental energies unhampered by discomfort.

This technique also has a healing quality. Anyone with some concentration can easily get rid of a headache, or even backache. Some sicknesses that are deeply rooted will be more difficult to eradicate, and indeed may be impossible to get rid of. But minor difficulties that are not chronic can be removed fairly easily. The technique has, however, many more possibilities.

One of its important aspects is that we learn to let go of feelings, so that we need not react. Feelings comprise physical sensations and emotions. The only doorway in the whole of worldly dependent arising through which we can step out of the wheel of birth and death is not to react to feelings, thereby letting go of craving. Craving always means "wanting to have" or "wanting to get rid of." We don't have to be addicts in the usual sense of the word; it's enough to want to keep or renew, destroy or reject. Here we have a method by which we can actually become aware of feelings, without any reaction being necessary. Even if anger arises, this is one occasion when we know with certainty that nobody has caused it. It has arisen, and this may be the first time in our life that we are aware of anger arising without any outside trigger. The same applies to grief, worry, fear, or any of our other emotions.

This method also gives us an opportunity to become aware of sensations that at times are unpleasant. If we drop them and move our attention to the next part of our body, we perform exactly the same action—namely, nonreaction to an unpleasant sensation by letting go of rejection. We are letting go by putting our attention elsewhere.

This method teaches us to deal with all our feelings with equanimity. We can tell ourselves over and over again that this is the only way to deal with emotions, and yet without training, we won't be able to follow through with it. Understanding—being intellectually aware—is the first step, but unless we have a way of practice, we can't learn that or any other skill.

I like to compare our emotions to a child's toy, a jack-in-the-box, which consists of a little doll mounted on a spring inside a box. The child just needs to touch the lid of the box lightly, and the little doll jumps out. Then someone pulls the little doll right out of the box. When the child now touches the lid, the doll won't appear. So the child gets a hammer and pounds on the lid, but the doll still won't come out. This is what is happening inside us. All our emotions are embedded in our hearts. We only need the slightest trigger, to be touched lightly, and anger or fear or passion jump out. When these are eventually gone, even pounding with a hammer will not induce them to reappear.

The purification we are aiming for needs a pathway. Naturally, we can practice in our daily lives where we are so often confronted by emotional reactions, but a method of meditation is an enormous aid and support system. First of all, this is because there is no outer "trigger," and it therefore becomes quite obvious that it is all happening within us. In the peace and quiet of meditation practice it is also much easier not to react than in the immediacy of confrontation—in the heat of the battle, so to speak.

Here we also have a method of gaining insight in various ways. During the guided meditation I mentioned hardness, warmth, movement. All bodies consist of the four primary elements, and these can easily be experienced in this particular meditation method. The primary elements are earth, water, fire, and air. Earth is the element of solidity, the hardness that we can feel when we touch the body, or when the body touches the cushion, floor, or chair. The water element is not only saliva, urine, sweat, and blood, but also the binding element. When we take some flour and pour water into it, it becomes dough. That is why about seventy-eight percent of our body is made up of water. If that were not so, all our parts would move about separately. We would look somewhat peculiar, but we might not have such a strong ego sense if we could actually observe all our separate cells. Water keeps our body together. The fire element is temperature; our body feels warm, cold, or medium. Then there is air, which is the winds in the body—the breath, and all physical movement.

When we experience any or all of these elements within us, we have a very good opportunity to relate that experience to everything around us. Everything that exists consists of these four elements, and each one of them contains the other three in varying proportions. For instance, water has to have solidity, otherwise we could neither swim in it nor paddle a boat over it. Even air has solidity, otherwise birds and airplanes couldn't fly. Gaining insight into ourselves as consisting of these elements helps us to realize that we are no different from our environment. No matter where we look, we find the elements of earth, fire, water, and air. As we fix our attention on this reality, our feeling of separation will diminish, giving us a greater sense of being part of the whole manifestation in this universe. We can feel embedded in this totality and no longer threatened by other people, or by natural or manmade catastrophes. We are part of the whole, the whole is part of us; there is no separation, no alienation.

The more we can live in this realization, the easier it is to purify our emotions with loving-kindness. When we no longer feel separated from others, a single unit among so many, but see only one universal manifestation, it becomes much easier to have loving-kindness for others, because essentially we are directing it toward ourselves.

When we observe ourselves in the light of the four primary elements, we also lose some of our deeply ingrained ego consciousness, which is the cause of each and every problem that can ever arise. It is impossible to find the attribute "me" in a combination of earth, water, fire, and air. Therefore, a contemplative inquiry into these aspects of ourselves can yield far-reaching results.

We all know about impermanence and have probably heard the word many times. There are few people in the world who will argue about impermanence, whether they are practicing a particular spiritual discipline or not. We could probably ask our postman or the man in the corner shop whether everything is impermanent, and they would surely agree that it is so. We all agree, but we have to experience impermanence before it makes an impact on us, and even then, that is not always enough. But the more often we do experience impermanence, the more often our mind turns from the ordinary way of thinking to the Dhamma way, which is a turnabout of 180 degrees. The latter is the reason why we have great difficulty in thinking about and living in the way of the Dhamma. But eventually, if we persevere long enough, are determined enough, and receive a little help on the way, it is possible. As we turn away from worldly thinking, impermanence becomes one of the outstanding features in everything we experience. In this meditation method we focus on the impermanence of every feeling and every sensation, and on their arising and cessation.

Not only do we experience their impermanence, but we also realize that we can only know whatever we fix our attention on. If we take that realization into our daily affairs, life becomes much easier. We do not have to put our attention on things that are troublesome, making life difficult for ourselves. When we experience negativity, we do not need to keep that in our consciousness. We are free to move our attention to that which is absolutely true, namely impermanence, unsatisfactoriness, and corelessness. Or we can relate to the pure emotions of loving-kindness, compassion, joy with others, and equanimity. It is entirely up to us where our attention is focused. As an outcome of meditation we learn that we can choose what to think, which is a new and valuable approach to our states of mind. This is also how we can eventually change our consciousness into Dhamma consciousness at all times. We will have learned to let go of those thoughts that are not in line with absolute truth.

The impermanence of our feelings and sensations, experienced during meditation, should give rise to insight into the impermanent nature of our whole being. That this body seems so solid in its form and shape is just a manifestation of the earth element, and is actually nothing but an optical illusion. When we experience feelings and sensations as totally impermanent, knowing that we usually live reacting to them, we begin to see ourselves as a little less solid than before, and may begin to question where "me" can be found within this constant change. This gives us an opportunity to place less importance on our feelings, just as we learn to consider our thoughts less important when we label them in meditation practice and see of how little use they are—that they are actually unsatisfactory, because they are constantly moving, changing, and disturbing.

Most people react automatically to their emotions and justify it by asserting that it is simply how they feel. We've all done that. There are bumper stickers in America that proclaim, "If it feels good, it must be right." That's not only foolish but dangerous.

We can see from all this how much importance is attached to feelings. As long as our consciousness has not yet become Dhamma consciousness, we will all fall into that trap. Now we have an opportunity for a new approach. Feelings are impermanent and entirely dependent upon where we fix our attention. How can they have any real significance beyond their rise and decline? Naturally, we won't always remember to adopt this new approach, but at least we have a method for dealing with our emotions that will eventually become part of our being. When we sit quietly and nothing is happening, it is easier to learn new methods for dealing with ourselves. In fact, it is not difficult at all to let go of one feeling and attend to another. But we need to be able to take that ability into the office and the kitchen when somebody scolds us, or demands attention. When we have done it over and over again in meditation, it becomes just as easy to do it in the office or the kitchen. We no longer have to be trapped by our feelings and by our reactions to them.

This attitude brings us to that point in dependent arising that is the doorway out of the realm of birth and death: namely, the practice of equanimity in response to feelings, instead of the customary "like" and "dislike," more succinctly called "greed" and "hate." Through awareness we will learn to make the right kind of choice. If we choose Dhamma, we will find ease and harmony within.

QUESTIONS

STUDENT: *Are you saying that if you have an itch in your eye, for instance, and then turn your attention to your fingers, you would not feel that itch in your eye?*

AYYA KHEMA: If you have enough concentration to drop the itch and attend to your fingers, yes. We often do that in meditation. If there is an itch somewhere, and we realize it is occupying our thoughts, we take our attention off it and go back to concentrating on the breath. If we are able to stay with the breath, the itch will take care of itself. We certainly all have the potential to learn this skill.

S: *Should this meditation always be done in the order that you described, starting from the top and going through each part like that?*

AK: Yes. Starting from the top and going down to the feet would be the natural progression. But you don't have to try to remember whether right or left arm comes first; that doesn't matter.

S: *A question came up about meditating while emotionally upset, and you replied that that was difficult to do and that it would be better to make a contemplative exploration of where the emotions came from. Suppose emotions arise while following this method; are you saying that by moving on, anger (or whatever emotion it is) would simply be left behind? Because the attention is no longer on that place, would the emotion also pass?*

AK: Yes, it would. However, it is very common for us to react. The anger may become the focus of attention, and one is unable to let go. We need to drop the whole emotional entanglement and go on to the next spot. Dropping is letting go, and the same emotional response may never arise again. If it is very deep seated, it may arise a second time. In that case we repeat the mental action of letting go. At such a time there is no need to investigate the origin of emotion.

S: *The method is to let go and move on to the next spot, keeping our attention on the method, so that we do not focus on anger or other emotions?*

AK: We must fully acknowledge that anger has come up, then let it go, and move on to the next spot. Sometimes it may take a while to be able to let go.

S: *This may be off the point, but it also has to do with strong emotions. Speaking of anger, I've noticed that, although one can drop the thoughts so as not to pay attention to the "trigger," there can still be some residue that seems to want to give birth to the same thoughts again. It's like energy, or a physical feeling.*

AK: It's an inner irritation; we have been stirred up and haven't smoothed that out yet. Here the same would also apply: take the attention off that irritated feeling, and instead put it on a feeling of loving-kindness for oneself or for someone for whom one can easily feel loving-kindness. In other words, change the focus of attention. If we keep our attention on the irritation, it may actually give rise to anger again. We need to realize that this is not wholesome, so we will substitute.

S: *It sounds a bit like when a young child is crying, and all one has to do is tell the child to look somewhere else, and the child drops the whole matter. So are you saying that we are the same?*

AK: Yes.

S: *I would like to ask you which aspects of your talk you feel would be most useful in terms of our daily lives and working situations. I am always really tense, which often comes from doing a lot of hard physical labor. I was wondering if you would suggest working with this method to relieve tension.*

AK: Do you feel physically tense because you have mental tension?

S: *No, but I find that when I do get emotionally tense it is much harder to relax if I've been working hard.*

AK: The best use you can make of this method is to follow it every day; I would like to suggest to everyone to use this method at least once a day. We need this internal purification regularly, like taking a shower every morning. If your concentration on this method is better than concentration on the breath, use it in all your meditation sittings. Methods are methods by any name. The concentration that comes with this method brings us to the same point that concentration on the breath does.

You can acknowledge the feeling that arises in you, which you call tension, and then take your mind off that and put it on loving-kindness, compassion, or joy with others, which means dropping the tension. If you don't feel love for yourself, use a person you are really fond of, or share joy with somebody who has just had good fortune or someone who feels compassion for everybody's suffering.

When tension takes over, you can also investigate its cause. The most likely cause is fear. When we know the cause, we can try to eliminate the underlying reasons. That is a contemplative effort, not particularly connected with this method, but also very useful.

S: *Where does this method of meditation come from?*

AK: This is a method that we could call mindfulness of feeling, the second base of mindfulness. It has been transmitted to us through Burmese teachers and meditation centers. These methods are an elaboration of what the Buddha taught.

S: *When I delve into my emotions, I don't accept or reject them. In the Tibetan tradition, we say that thought and emotion are self-liberating. They are not seen as something obstructive.*

AK: The recognition of them without reaction is self-liberating.

S: *Yes, that's right. It may take a while to reach that point because we may be knocked off the track. On one hand, we are talking about vipassanā, which seems like a great contemplation exercise in which we can examine our emotions and their causes, and try to get down to the essence in that way. And on the other, we are actually practicing awareness. I am trying to clarify all these little aspects of your tradition and our [Tibetan] tradition, and to be clear about what they mean.*

AK: May I suggest that you just take in what you hear, and try to practice. Having practiced, you won't have the problem you are having now. After a few days the answers will be quite clear to you, because you've actually experienced them. Afterward you can easily bring the two traditions together.

The next time we sit, everybody can use this method on their own, and then you will have a clearer idea of what it means to become aware of feelings and sensations, and letting go of them. Use your own pace when going through the body by yourself. Did anyone have no feelings or sensations at all?

S: *I had pain...in my back and in my chest; a lot of pain. But it has been there all the time. I am kind of aware of it anyway.*

AK: Can you feel your lips on top of one another?

S: *Yes. I felt physically aware of all the parts of my body, but nothing else came up. I have too much pain; I can't feel anything other than the pain.*

AK: You are unable to let go of the pain, even for a moment?

S: *I have been trying for two days now.*

AK: Is your pain constant? When you get up, is it still there?

S: *Well, it's still there, but the longer I sit, the worse it gets. So then I carry it around with me.*

AK: When you sit down, do you get the pain immediately?

S: *Not immediately. It just gets worse and worse the longer I sit.*

AK: I would suggest that you practice this method early in the morning, and continue with it as long as you can. If there's that much pain, you won't be able to pay attention to the breath either. I will show you something specific that will either make the pain bearable or eliminate it.

S: *I got a headache when we were practicing this method.*

AK: Headaches can be of two kinds. One kind develops when one tries too hard, and the effort creates tension. The other kind of headache comes if one thinks too much, instead of meditating.

S: *That happens with me. I get slight headaches because in order to facilitate the process, I imagine the back or the palm of my hand. And my concentration is on the imagined image and not on my actual back or hand.*

AK: That's a very complicated process.

S: *Yes; I do it automatically, and I know it's not what I am supposed to be doing. How can I stop it? I suppose I have a visual mind that just jumps to it.*

AK: Can't you put your visual mind on the hand as it really is?

S: *I do that sometimes, but the image jumps back. There's this leap back and forth, from feeling and sensation, and also this energy...*

AK: Yes. I understand what you are experiencing, but it's unusual, because most people with visual minds can first visualize and then get the feeling. When there is no feeling, that's when the image jumps back into your mind.

S: *It's electric—it happens so quickly. As soon as I move on from spot to spot, I could jump back into another image instead of on to the spot, so I am always constructing the image.*

AK: Couldn't you visualize your body parts as if you were painting them on a canvas right at the place where the part is? Try doing that, and stay with the body part to get the feeling.

S: *I think I know what you mean. I am experimenting with this, with enveloping my actual body parts with my image of them. But sometimes that dissolves into concentrating on the top of my hand, or whatever.*

AK: That's much too complicated. Use a straightforward approach. You know where your body is and what it looks like. You have a visual mind, so get it to visualize an arm as it really is, then go along that arm as it really is, and experience the feeling. You are complicating your meditation quite unnecessarily.

S: *Can this particular practice be done lying down?*

AK: When you wake up, you'll know why not! That would be conducive to going to sleep.

S: *My problem is that when I want to do this, I tend to stray. My thoughts just lead me astray. I pull them back and start again from the head, but I hardly ever complete the whole body.*

AK: When you become distracted and then resume the meditation, always go back to approximately where you stopped. Do not start with the head over and over again.

S: *Isn't there a Theravāda method in which, instead of diverting the attention, you actually put one-pointed attention on the feeling, whether it's physical pain or anger?*

AK: The Buddha taught that first we learn to substitute, and when we don't need to substitute any longer we are able to drop anger or pain immediately. The third stage is when anger gradually subsides to the point where there is no anger left within us. First substitution, then dropping, and then gradual purification. The Buddha also taught that the more often we allow ourselves to be angry, the deeper the ruts of anger will be in the mind; it becomes therefore more and more difficult to eliminate it because it is so deeply embedded. The minute anger arises, we should deal with it as best we can.

S: *I was unable to move from point to point. I didn't have the concentration. I was only able to concentrate as far as the head. Then I was angry because of my lack of skill, and the anger became the focus.*

AK: Were you able to drop the anger?

S: *No.*

AK: Did you keep it all the way through the meditation?

S: *Yes...I think so.*

AK: Did you find a scapegoat, somebody whose fault this was?

S: *I blamed myself; I was the scapegoat.*

AK: That is just as unwholesome as it is to blame someone else. The idea is to accept the anger and be able to substitute a wholesome emotion.

S: *I didn't think of that.*

AK: In order for the method to work, we have to remember how to do it.

S: *Would you substitute loving-kindness right in the middle of meditation?*

AK: Yes. When you are unable to substitute attention on the subject of meditation, anger must be replaced by loving-kindness as quickly as possible. In order to benefit from the Buddha's teachings, we need to take three steps. We need to first obtain the instructions, then remember them, and finally put them into practice. Having done that, we gain insight from our practice.

Did anybody feel nauseated during the guided meditation? It is one of the strongest reactions one can get and results from good concentration.

S: *I thought I was going to vomit, actually.*

AK: Nobody ever does, but the feeling of wanting to vomit is a significant cleansing, comparable to carrying a lot of rubbish outside all at once. It will most likely not occur again. It is considered a very distinctive aspect of purification. Did anybody have not only sensations but also emotional feelings?

S: *I didn't feel anger, but a sense of great space and sadness.*

AK: That's very useful, because the more these buried emotions come out, the more they dissolve into nothingness. When they remain within, they coalesce into difficulties. The more we clean out, the less burdened we become.

S: *I felt that my two sides were different—not exactly a division between them, just different. One side seemed very spacious, the other seemed flat.*

AK: When you use this method again, investigate whether you feel anything that might be a barrier. If you do, I will tell you how to deal with it.

S: *I feel volume everywhere.*

AK: We always need to differentiate between thinking and feeling. How do we feel volume? We can feel solidity and compactness. We can feel hardness, or even size. We can have an actual feeling of dimension. Some people don't feel anything on their skin; they have to start with touch, such as the touch of their clothes. Then feeling the skin follows, and later they can feel what is within, such as softness or hardness, or other sensations. When we feel size, there is a boundary, and there is content of various modes.

S: *I keep going from the feeling to my image of it. That's my problem. I jump back and forth. I am aware of my arm, and at the same time I am aware of the image I have in my mind.*

AK: Increased concentration will solve that.

S: *I think that I am impatient. I want to finish.*

AK: You might have a notion of achievement, which is quite common. We do the best we can and have as much awareness as possible, that's all. There is nothing to achieve, not even anything to finish. There is no right or wrong; there is only knowing.

⫷ 8 Joy

Step 3

THE THIRD STEP IN THE SEQUENCE of transcendental dependent arising is joy. Dependent arising means that we recognize cause and effect. The first step of realizing unsatisfactoriness did not just imply that we are confronted with suffering, but that we know what it actually means: namely, that it is part of existence, inherent in all manifestation, and that the world cannot alter in that respect. From that understanding grow faith and confidence in the spiritual life, and as a result, joy arises. These three are necessary preconditions for meditation.

The joy that we are discussing here comes from confidence in a spiritual path, from having found a way that will lead out of worldly problems and that promises total liberation and release. That joy should be strong enough not to alter whether external conditions are pleasant or not, because we know already that external conditions only concern our sense contacts. Unless we are clear on this point, we will vacillate repeatedly—whether we should continue on this spiritual path, get married, go to university, take a trip to China, or have a vegetable garden. Unless this precondition of inner joy is fulfilled, we cannot be certain whether practice is the only thing that can take us out of unsatisfactoriness. We need to realize, without a shadow of a doubt, that everything else consists of sense contacts, which can only provide momentary pleasure, without any lasting value. They come and they go. That doesn't mean that sense contacts are inherently bad, or that they can be avoided. The Buddha described them as being of a gross nature.

Once we realize that our sense contacts cannot satisfy us, we need to investigate whether there is anything apart from them to be found in this world. When we have arrived at an understanding of the unsatisfactory nature of our senses, there is no question about being joyful about our spiritual path. This inner joy is an absolute necessity for successful meditation. We can easily verify this through our own experience. Meditation only works when there is an inner feeling of no bother, no problem, no worry, no wish.

The Buddha's explanations about meditation often start out with "secluded," but that word is frequently misunderstood and thought to mean that we have to seclude ourselves from the world and abandon all human contact. It doesn't mean that at all. It means "secluded from sense contacts." Being secluded from sense contacts, we can start meditating, but in order to fulfill that condition there has to be an inner feeling of happiness, of ease, of contentment; a knowing that we are doing the best possible thing, otherwise, thinking will interrupt us again and again. If we have inner joy, not only will we continue on our path, and meditation will work for us, but we will be able to retain the joy all the time. It doesn't only arise when we sit down on the cushion or when we remember something about our spiritual practice. It is part and parcel of our inner being, as a certainty of having found the way out of human problems. That we haven't actually reached the end of this pathway yet doesn't matter.

Happiness is the aim of every being. In this spiritual teaching we have been shown a way, like a map to reach a destination. It's a destination that we all want to reach, but we don't know exactly what it looks like or what to expect. Isn't it a great cause for joy, gratitude, and devotion to have received such a detailed road map with the promise of fulfilling our dearest wish? It must give rise to a feeling of being blessed. Until that feeling develops, meditation is going to be an off-and-on affair. It need not be that. Once established, it can progress steadily. When meditation becomes steady, it is a great jewel that we can carry around with us.

Joy can arise from this cause alone—from knowing that we have been given a pathway that we can follow and that we can trust, because it has already been a blessing to many who have reached their goal that way. But there are other means of arousing joy in ourselves. Joy is not pleasure. Pleasure comes from the senses and is short-lived. It doesn't mean we should never have pleasure; it will arise from sense contacts until equanimity becomes strongly established. But pleasure and joy are two entirely different emotions. We can assist ourselves on our path by creating joy through making good karma—such as, for instance, deliberately making ourselves available to others. When our intention is to help and support others and we turn our full attention to that, problems of our own cannot arise at that time because our attention is engaged elsewhere. Being able to do something for others, whether gratitude is forthcoming or not, arouses joy in the heart. Contentment and satisfaction come from knowing that one has done one's utmost.

The Buddha mentions ten virtues[7] that we need to cultivate and foster. At the top of the list is generosity. Generosity includes giving one's time, attention, love, and compassion, creating some happiness for others. When we can actually see that this has happened, joy in our heart is a natural outcome. Even when the other person's happiness is not apparent, yet we know we have given of our best, it is impossible not to feel joyful. Joy also comes from knowing that one is keeping discipline, which must always be self-discipline. Imposed discipline is irksome and can seem like a chain, and one will automatically resist and reject it, or feel hampered by it. Whatever discipline we are keeping, we are imposing it upon ourselves, and we can rejoice in the fact that we are conquering ourselves.

The Buddha said, "The one who conquers a thousand times a thousand armies is like nothing compared to the one who conquers him- or herself." Our instincts go against self-conquest and are constantly reaching out toward pleasures of the senses.

The gratification of our senses is the first and foremost consideration we have in everything we experience. Conquering some of that instinctual reaction means we can rejoice in being a warrior on our way to liberation. This should not be construed to mean that we are engaged in a battle, which is fearsome and unpleasant, but it reflects our need to be courageous and self-reliant, honest about ourselves to ourselves. Courage and honesty give us strength to impose self-discipline. All of that brings joy to our hearts, the joy of knowing that we are actually moving away from ordinary problematic human life, which we have already tasted to its fullest, and yet have never resolved to our satisfaction. Knowing that we have found a different direction gives us a joyful resolve to continue without hesitation.

There's a story about the Buddha at the time before his enlightenment, when he was still the Bodhisattva. He had been fasting and had realized that extreme asceticism was not conducive to clarity of mind. His path is therefore often called "the middle way." The story tells us that he had sat down under what we now call a bodhi tree in present-day Bodhgaya in northern India.

It was known in the area that there was a *deva* living in that tree who could be helpful to those wishing to conceive a child. A woman named Sujata had been praying to the tree *deva* to help her have a baby, and her prayers had been answered. She sent out her maid to start preparing an offering to the *deva*, which she had promised in her prayers. When the maid came to the tree, she saw the Bodhisattva sitting under it and thought it was the tree *deva*. She ran home to her mistress and told her that the tree *deva* was sitting under the tree. Sujata decided to hurry with the offering, to meet the *deva* in person.

The story relates that she first milked a hundred cows and gave the milk to fifty cows to drink. Then she milked the fifty cows and gave that milk to twenty cows. Next she milked the twenty cows and gave the milk to ten cows, and then she milked the ten cows and gave the milk to one cow. When she milked the last cow, it gave forth pure cream. She then cooked rice in this pure cream, and filled a golden bowl with it. She took the rice in the golden bowl to the tree, to what she thought was the tree *deva*. She offered the rice to him, and asked that he keep the golden bowl too. The Bodhisattva ate the rice (which in Sinhalese is called *kiribat*, meaning "milk rice," served in Sri Lanka to this day on all holy or festive occasions).

When the Bodhisattva had finished his meal, he took the golden bowl and said he would throw it into the river behind him. If it floated downstream, he would not become enlightened. But if it floated upstream, against the current, he would become the Buddha. Obviously, it must have floated upstream, although one cannot imagine a golden bowl doing that.

However, this is a symbolic story, and one that is quite important for us. It means that following the Dhamma is like swimming upstream. Swimming downstream with the current is much easier; everybody goes in that direction. But we end up in the mudflats. When we swim upstream against the current, we are more or less alone and have to work much harder, but we arrive at the clean and unpolluted source. The source of a river is always upstream. It is our good fortune to know the path and the direction. We have to take into account that it is much more difficult to go against the stream, instead of going along with the rest of humanity, because it also means resisting our own instincts and impulses.

Whenever desires and ideas arise and the joy of the path momentarily disappears, we can remember that this is natural, instinctive human behavior, from which we are trying to sever ourselves. Every time we succeed even a little, we find renewed joy in our spiritual practice. We understand the path and its beauty, and we realize that many others before us have been able to reach their goal by swimming against the stream. We also have a feeling of extending our power and strength, because we are not giving in. Everyone has some particular skill that can be used in spiritual practice. Some people find it easy to be calm and collected, others are good at analysis; some have a good memory, others are skillful writers. We need to use all our existing abilities and extend them to the fullest.

The Buddha recommended simplicity in thought, word, and deed, because our minds are convoluted enough, and the more complicated our thought process, the more difficult we find it to practice. The simplicity of his explanations can add to our joy as part of our everyday experience, the joy of being in the right place at the right time, and acting in the right way with our whole being.

There are five spiritual faculties which, when fully developed, turn into powers; as such, they become factors of enlightenment. These five faculties—mindfulness, faith, wisdom, energy, and concentration—are compared to a team of horses with a lead horse and two pairs. The lead horse can go as fast or as slowly as it likes, but the two pairs have to balance or the cart will topple.

The lead horse is mindfulness, a faculty we all have (otherwise, we would be run over the first time we crossed a street!). However, we need to develop mindfulness further to make it into a power. This entails remembering to use it when walking, standing, sitting, when opening a door or closing it, when performing any action with body or mind. Naturally, we will forget at times, but when the mind says, "I have forgotten to be mindful," that is the moment when we remember again. Without mindfulness we will not become aware of the joy within us, because we habitually look for gratification through our sense contacts. Mindfully we know that we have had many sensual gratifications in this life, and that none of them has ever fulfilled its promise; so it isn't necessary to look for another one.

Instead, we can observe our actions, our movements, our feelings, and our thoughts. Mindfulness is our leading quality, an objective introspection, with no judgmental overtones. Without that, we are in constant danger of being drowned by emotions, or buffeted by unskillful reactions.

The first pair of horses that have to go together are faith and wisdom. Faith leads us to devotion, to total commitment, and wisdom lets us know whether we are devoted and committed to the truth. Unless we have that assurance, our faith could be ill placed.

The second pair are energy and concentration. If we have too much energy, it results in mental and physical restlessness, which most people experience at some time or other. If there is a great deal of physical energy, the restlessness needs to be counteracted by physical activity. If there is too much mental energy, resulting in agitated thinking, we can use that constructively by giving direction to our thoughts. If we have too much concentration, energy will lapse, and there will be a lack of awareness. Too much concentration can also lead to drowsiness, so we need to balance between them constantly. This is a very typical aspect of the Buddha's path. It is a balancing act of loving oneself and being there for others, of using energy so that concentration may develop, of balancing faith and wisdom so that heart and mind cooperate, bringing together what we know and what we feel. Unless we use the Dhamma in the right way, it will be like a snake. When picked up by the tail, it can bite us; held behind the head, there is no danger. "Spiritual materialism" is one of the best descriptions of that danger.

When heart and mind are balanced, the mind understands what we are doing, and the heart can feel. The spiritual path can only be practiced through our feelings. If we understand the teaching but don't feel any benefit, it is an intellectual exercise and belongs at the university. What we are engaged in is the arousing of profoundly felt insights which can change us from an ordinary worldling into a noble one—one who has personal experience of liberation. Joy is a necessary inner feeling if we are to follow this path. If we don't enjoy our practice, why should we do it? Very few people would continue something they don't enjoy and don't consider beautiful and valuable. Inner joy need never be marred by outer circumstances. As long as we are dependent on outer circumstances, we are victims without freedom of choice. This path leads to complete freedom. We need to find the inner strength to be dependent on nothing except what we can arouse in ourselves.

QUESTIONS

STUDENT: *Isn't the attachment to the senses the problem, rather than the senses themselves?*

AYYA KHEMA: The senses themselves are, of course, not a problem, because we cannot live without them. But it is the mind's explanations of them that creates the problem. I will tell you a story to illustrate this.

There was a married couple who one day had a big argument. The wife decided she was going to leave; she'd had enough. She put on all her best saris, one on top of the other, and all her golden jewelry, and ran away. After a while her husband repented and decided to go after her to bring her back. He hurried to catch up with her but couldn't find her. As he hurried along a village road, he saw a monk walking by. He stopped the monk and said, "Sir, have you seen a pretty woman with long black hair, wearing a red sari and a lot of golden jewelry, coming along this road?"

The monk said, "I saw a set of teeth going by."

Although the monk saw the woman, he did not start to explain to himself that this was a pretty woman with long black hair, a red sari, and golden jewelry. He knew how to calm his senses down to the point where he only saw teeth going by. It is not our senses that are the problem; we need them and can't live very well without them. We would have a very difficult life if we were blind or deaf. The problem lies with our ideation.

S: *I think taking that view literally would lead to a lack of appreciation. For instance, my experience of joy is that my appreciation of everything is intensified. The birds and the ocean and the sunlight are more beautiful. It's not the same as attachment, but more a sense of rejoicing in the beauty of things...I don't know how to express it.*

AK: Yes, I understand what you are saying. The distinction that is made, though, is that we can have inner joy independent of sense contacts. Sense contacts cannot be avoided, and they may result in appreciation of beauty, but try not to be dependent upon beauty for inner joy; don't wait for a "trigger" for joy to arise. Beauty does happen, but we can experience the impermanence of our sense contacts and also realize that a bird's life contains much unsatisfactoriness.

Joy comes from our inner understanding that, because of impermanence, there is nothing to hang on to, nothing to worry about, nowhere to go, nothing to be done.

The Buddha described sense contacts as being like a cow that has been skinned alive, and flies are settling on the bare flesh all the time. There is constant irritation for that cow. In the same way, sense contacts are a source of irritation, because the mind is perpetually engaged in trying to explain them. A bird's singing is nothing but sound, but the mind makes up stories about every sound we hear. Having realized the limitations of the senses, we will look for fulfillment within, and not outside.

S: *Is there something that you could call "pure perception"?*

AK: There was a man called Bahia at the time of the Buddha. Bahia had been a religious teacher for thirty years and thought he was enlightened. One night a *deva* came to him and said to him, "Bahia, you're not enlightened. You don't even know how to become enlightened." (The *deva* may have been an intuition.) Bahia became quite perturbed and said, "What, I'm not enlightened, I don't know how? How can I learn?" The *deva* said, "You have to go and see the Buddha. He will tell you how to become enlightened."

Bahia immediately left his house to find the Buddha. The next morning he arrived at the village where the Buddha was and went to the house where he was staying. He had gone on alms round. The people in the house told Bahia, "Don't ask him questions now, he's gone on alms round and won't answer." But Bahia was so keen to find out how to become enlightened that he didn't listen to their advice.

He ran after the Buddha and found him in the village. He greeted him respectfully, and said, "Sir, I want to ask you a question." The Buddha answered, "You've come at the wrong time for questions; I'm on alms round." But Bahia would not be deterred and asked him again, receiving the same answer. Bahia asked a third time (in Indian tradition, a teacher cannot refuse if a student requests spiritual help three times), and the Buddha said, "Well, what is it? What do you want to know?"

Bahia said, "I want to know how to become enlightened." The Buddha replied, "For you, Bahia, the seen is only the seen, the heard is only the heard, the known is only the known." Bahia thanked him and walked away.

In the afternoon the Buddha went for a walk with his monks and they found Bahia dead by the side of the road. A runaway calf had killed him, and the Buddha said, "Bahia was enlightened before he died."

The Buddha's one sentence was enough for Bahia, after thirty years of practice, to realize what enlightenment meant. To recognize the "seen as only the seen, the heard as only the heard, the known as only the known" means to experience sense contacts as nothing substantial, not owned by us, needing no reaction, and as only a passing show.

✺❘9 Concentration: The Meditative Absorptions

Step 4

Next in our sequence of transcendental dependent arising come the meditation steps. We have to understand that meditation as a whole is a means to an end and not an end in itself. This is particularly true of the meditative absorptions (*jhāna*). At the time of the Buddha meditation was well established in India. The Buddha's contribution, however, was his realization that concentration was not sufficient; then, as now, it was a widespread belief that the eight meditative absorptions, when perfected, were all that can be achieved on the spiritual path, and were equivalent to becoming one with atman, the all-pervading essence. The Buddha himself practiced and perfected these meditation states, while staying with his two teachers, for six years. He struck out on his own then, because he realized he had not yet come to the end of the path, but he could find no other teacher to instruct him in insight. It is said that all buddhas discover that insight for themselves, and that it takes exactly the same form.

It is essential not to fall into the error of believing that practicing tranquility is unnecessary because insight is the goal. This, too, is a widespread and erroneous belief, and it is not based on the Buddha's actual instructions. In discourse after discourse he deals with the path of practice to come from our worldly state to liberation, and the meditative absorptions are part of that path. They are a necessary means to this end because through them the mind acquires the ability to be one-pointed, to have enough strength to stay quietly in one spot.

Without that mental power the mind cannot penetrate the depth and profundity of the Buddha's teaching, where ultimate, absolute truth can be found. Lacking strength, it cannot pierce the layers of illusion but wobbles from one thought to the next. The mind not yet equipped with one-pointedness can gain some insights on a more superficial level, which will help it to become more concentrated.

There is another aspect to the efficacy of the meditative absorptions, which is demonstrated at the very outset of the practice. The first meditative absorption has five factors, or attributes, which counteract our five hindrances in an automatic process. Once we are able to gain access to the first meditative absorption, we are provided with a purification system, which of course also needs support in daily living. This fact alone should provide enough impetus for our concentration.

The five hindrances that the Buddha enumerated are the difficulties that beset every worldling. None of us is immune, and they only slowly and gradually disappear.

The first meditative factor occurs in any meditation, whether absorbed or not; in Pali it is called *vitakka*, which means "initial application," or fixing one's mind on the subject of meditation. Whether this is successful or not, initial application arises every time we try to meditate. This mental action counteracts the third of the hindrances, namely sloth and torpor. When there is sloth and torpor, the mind has no strength at all, not even enough wakefulness to fix itself on the subject of meditation. The more often we put our mind to the subject of meditation, the more we counteract torpor. A mind without clarity also creates sloth in the body; however, it is the mind in particular that we are addressing through the meditation process. The mind that says, "I'll do it later," "I'll do it tomorrow," "It can't be that important," "I'm a bit tired now," "I can't really be bothered," or "I wonder whether there is any use in doing it" is looking for any excuse it can find to avoid meditating. Our minds are habit prone, and it is very difficult to get out of old habits. Establishing new habits means giving ourselves a push, which must not be too hard or too gentle. It has to be balanced, and only we ourselves know where that balance lies.

If initial application does not give rise to sustained application, discursive thinking will follow it. This is exactly what happens in the meditation process when there is no real concentration and nothing to rely on. The initial mind thrust has to be followed by the next meditative factor, called in Pali *vicāra*. These first two are always mentioned together because meditation is only possible when they are joined. *Vicāra* means "sustained application," a description of a mind that is no longer veering off the subject of meditation but staying with it, maintaining concentration. Everybody knows that meditation only works when one can keep the mind on the subject of meditation, but the various difficulties that arise are not always familiar.

The second meditative factor, sustained application, counteracts skeptical doubt. When we can stay with the subject of meditation and do not become distracted, we gain confidence through the experience that, first of all, it is possible; secondly, that we are able to do it; and thirdly, that the results that accrue are exactly as the Buddha said. Until then, doubt arises again and again in the most insidious ways. Skeptical doubt is the enemy of faith and confidence, and therefore of practice; the mind can provide all sorts of ideas, doubts, and excuses—"There must be an easier way," or "I'll try something different," or "I'll find a better teacher or a better monastery," or "There must be something that will really grip me." The mind is a magician: it can produce a rabbit out of any hat.

Skeptical doubt shows itself when we cannot fully immerse ourselves in our present situation. Skeptical doubt keeps us back, because we are afraid to lose control or self-importance. When we have a little personal experience of the results of the Buddha's teachings, our doubts are counteracted, yet not completely eliminated. At least we no longer feel unsure about practicing meditation. We have experienced results and we have also realized that it makes no difference where we practice, as long as we are steadfast. That, too, is important, because we can search for a perfect place, time, situation, or teacher until the end of our lives and never find any of these because skeptical doubt always intervenes.

Initial and sustained application are the first two factors of the meditative absorptions and can be likened to unlocking the door to concentration. All the meditation methods we use are simply keys. There are no good or bad keys, but if we hold a key in our hand long and steadily enough, we will eventually be able to fit it into a keyhole. Turning the key in the keyhole opens the door, which gives us access to what we might call a house with eight rooms. As we step into the entry hall, which the first two meditative factors allow us to do, we can go into the first room. If we continue to practice, eventually the key will be unnecessary, because the door will remain unlocked.

When we enter into the meditative absorptions the mind stretches and becomes pliable, soft, malleable, and expansive. If we stop again, naturally the mind shrinks back to its usual and shrunken limitations. We can compare this with practicing yoga exercises. When we stretch the body persistently we find we can touch our toes with no difficulty, because muscles and sinews have been made pliable. When we stop practicing for six months or so, we have to start all over again; the muscles shrink back to their former tightness.

To stretch the mind—to make it malleable, pliable, and expansive—is necessary in order to encompass the whole of the teachings. When the mind is still limited and shrunken in its capacity, though we live and survive, we will only be able to understand the Dhamma in a limited way. That is quite natural. The Buddha's path always consisted of study and practice. We must know the direction, but we have to practice to experience mind expansion. Only practice makes it possible to see with an inner vision a reality different from the one we are used to.

The third factor that arises after sustained application is called *pīti* in Pali, and "bliss" or "rapture" in English. It is an extremely pleasant physical feeling. People practicing meditation often experience this feeling without their knowing what to do with it. Meditation moves in that direction quite naturally. The mind yearns for release from constant thinking and longs to be peaceful and at ease, which is probably the reason for beginning to meditate. What other reasons do people usually have? Hardly any others, except to be able to stop thinking about past problems which could recur in the future, or are present now, and to become peaceful instead. The mind not only yearns for that but also has a subtle recognition that this is the direction it can follow.

Every mind is capable of utter peace and quiet; it is a matter of application and determination. If we apply ourselves and are determined to continue, there's no reason why anyone should not be able to follow this path. It is the natural progression for every human mind. The blissful feeling is a physical feeling, but the attention at that time is not on the body as such but only on the feeling. What actually happens in meditative practice is this: when we have been attentive to the breath and sustained the attention, the quality of the breath changes. It becomes finer and finer, because the mind has become one-pointed and inwardly directed. It no longer attends to outside matters, only to the breath. Finally the breath seems to vanish, becoming so imperceptible that the mind can hardly find it, or fails to find it altogether.

At that moment, initial and sustained application have been completed and bliss can follow. Seventeen types of pleasant feelings are listed. They are individually different and can also vary from one meditation session to another. Some of them consist of a lightness of the body, as if the body had become weightless. This feeling can be so strong that the person to whom it happens for the first time might look to see if they have risen from the cushion on which they are sitting. Sometimes there is tingling throughout the body, which feels very pleasant, or a feeling of growing taller, or the dimensions of the body may disappear altogether. Whatever the feeling may be, it is always extremely pleasant and therefore effectively counteracts ill will.

When we experience such a pleasant sensation and are able to sustain it (not just momentarily), and also resurrect it at will, then it naturally fills the mind with goodwill. How could one bear ill will toward anyone or anything in the face of this pleasant feeling?

This is one of the very important aspects of the ability to enter into the meditative absorptions: namely, that no matter what happens in one's daily life, independent of outside triggers and external conditions, the mind knows it can attain this pleasure, of which the Buddha said, "This is a pleasure I will allow myself." He contrasted it with the pleasures of the senses, which he deemed gross and dependent upon external conditions. When our pleasures and our joy depend on our sense contacts, we are the victims of outside conditions. Here we may experience the first instance of becoming master of our own situation. We no longer need any outside conditions; all we need is the inner condition of concentration. While this still remains in the realm of dependent arising, we are now, at least to some extent, independent of what goes on around us.

Even though we will still find irksome reactions within us, we nevertheless retain the knowledge that we can return to that place where the mind has found a home. We can compare this with a home for the body. If the body didn't have a roof over its head, a bed to sleep in, a place to shelter from rain, wind, storm, snow, or sun, but had to live, eat, and sleep on the street, we would be quite disturbed. The mind doesn't have such a home. While the body may be sitting peacefully in the most comfortable armchair, the mind can be distracted by the most violent problems. While the body has a roof over its head and is fully protected from all the inclemencies of the weather, the mind is by no means protected from the storms of its own emotions. It has no home where it can shelter. Its one desire is to fall asleep, because at least then it only dreams and so is not consciously aware of its problems.

When we are able to enter into the meditative absorptions, the mind has a home where it can retreat and be safe, for the duration of the meditation, from the storms of its emotions. Naturally, these emotions will gradually be purified, because such a pleasant abiding reduces one's ill will, which also can be called hate or dislike, anger, or resistance—any name will do, as long as we realize that every worldling suffers from these negative emotions.

The Buddha compared being angry with someone picking up hot coals with bare hands and trying to throw them at one's enemy. Who gets burnt first? The one who's picking up the coals, of course—the one who is angry. We may not even hit the target we are aiming at, because if that person is clever and practiced enough, he'll duck, and we shall have burnt hands. The Buddha also said that one who can check risen anger is a true practitioner, just as a charioteer who can check wild horses and bring them back to do their duty is a real charioteer.

This pleasant abiding that results from initial and sustained application to the subject of meditation automatically soothes our negative emotions. The negativities that develop from our reactions to outer "triggers" will not swamp and engulf us as completely as before. We shall still have to work with them as they arise in daily life, but they will be far less of a problem.

Another benefit accruing from meditative absorption is compassion. One naturally wants to help others to attain these states of pleasant abiding, which generate a smooth and harmonious inner life. We are all practiced at tidying and cleaning our rooms and we wouldn't like to live in a mess, but we also need to clean and tidy up our "inner household." An inner household that contains a lot of confusion and negative emotions is very difficult to live with, just as it is difficult to live in a household where everything is topsy-turvy. When we smooth out our difficulties, the ease of living becomes apparent. That doesn't mean that there is no more unsatisfactoriness. As long as there's an "I," there's unsatisfactoriness, but that inner ease greatly facilitates meditation.

A pleasant feeling is naturally accompanied by happiness, which counteracts the fourth hindrance, restlessness and worry. If we are happy in the present, we cannot worry at the same time; neither do we think of the future and its possible problems. One very important result of this meditative experience is that we no longer look for happiness to come to us from outside but realize that it depends solely upon our own efforts. Our worries about the future are totally absurd, because the one who worries does not remain the same person to experience that future. A glimpse into impermanence shows us that clearly. Continuity covers up impermanence but certainly doesn't alter the fact of it; again and again we are fooled into believing ourselves to be a solid entity. Restlessness also disappears, because having found what one wants, namely happiness, there is nothing to be restless about.

Where could one go to find anything better? As long as happiness still eludes us, we are restless wherever we are, because we are not fulfilled. If we have inner happiness, it no longer matters where we happen to be. Happiness resulting from the initial pleasant physical feeling eliminates restlessness and worry during meditation. Our hindrances are by no means uprooted, but they are certainly laid to rest while we meditate.

We can look at it in this way: if we have a garden full of weeds and let them grow as they please, they will eventually use up all the nourishment from the soil and completely overshadow the flowers and vegetables, taking away food, sun, and water from them. If the weeds have deep roots, as some have, and are therefore difficult to uproot, the only thing to do is to cut them down. As we cut them down, they become weaker and weaker, no longer using up all the nourishment and overshadowing the good plants. This is exactly what happens in meditation. We do not uproot the hindrances, but we cut them down. As we continue to cut them down again and again, they become so feeble and small that eventually it is no longer such an enormous task to uproot them. Of course, we must practice every day, because—as every gardener knows—weeds always grow more easily than flowers and vegetables; constant vigilance is needed in every garden, be it a physical one or the garden of our hearts and minds.

The fifth factor that arises at the time of the first meditative absorption is one-pointedness. As long as there is one-pointedness, one can remain concentrated. One-pointedness counteracts our desire for sensual gratification. Luckily, we are unable to do two things with our mind at the same time. When we are one-pointed and totally absorbed in a pleasant feeling or in happiness, we have no other desires. At such a time, any pain in the body is without significance. It is not an object of attention, so there is no wish for greater physical comfort. We don't look for other pleasant sense experiences, because a far greater pleasure than ever before is being experienced.

The first four meditative absorptions, of which I have just explained the first, are called the *rupajhāna*s. *Rupa* means body, materiality, corporeality. In English we can call them "fine-material absorptions," because all the states that arise are known to us in a similar, but far less refined, way. Although quantitatively and qualitatively of much less significance, these experiences are part of our makeup.

We have all experienced very pleasant bodily feelings. The ones arising in meditation are different and yet familiar, although superior in every way. When such feelings occur for the first time, people often shed tears of joy. However, the mind might say, "Goodness, what's that?" which effectively disrupts concentration so that one has to start all over again.

When the breath becomes so fine that it is almost impossible to detect, the pleasant physical feeling follows, and our attention is focused on it. When that dissipates, either because concentration lapses or the meditation is over, two things should be remembered before we open our eyes. We experience then and there the impermanence of even the most pleasant feelings. We have absolutely no objection to experiencing the impermanence of unpleasant feelings, but we have a great deal of objection to the impermanence of pleasant feelings. Yet both are equally impermanent. As we progress in insight we will see what an important factor it is to recognize the dissipation of this very pleasant feeling and actually watch it dissolve.

To watch the dissolution of one's subject of meditation is a further step in insight. First, we experience the arising and the ceasing; now in our meditation practice we can watch the disappearance. At that moment, the dissolution does not generate any dislike or unhappiness, because the mind still carries its meditative ease within. However, in the beginning a common reaction is, "What a pity! I hope I can get that feeling back." When the mind reacts in this way, we have to realize that this denotes attachment. We need to watch the dissolving of the pleasant feeling in the knowledge that this is a law of nature manifest before our own inner vision.

The second important point of attention is recapitulation. We need to resurrect all the steps we have taken in the whole of that meditation, so that eventually we can always follow that particular method of concentration. Everyone will find their own special trigger which is unique to them, although the meditation progression itself is universal for all human minds. One needs to remember whether any action or thought has been different this time, even before entering the meditation room: whether one has used a different posture, or, when starting the meditation, whether one has used a different meditation approach. Eventually, one will find the necessary trigger so that one can always enter the "first room" of this house with no difficulty at all just by sitting down in the meditative posture. The mind is habit prone; if it has done something often enough it will continue to do it, unless we deliberately change our mental habits.

In the beginning we need the necessary meditation practice, the methods that will be our key to open the door, but within them we must find something that is of particular help to us. That element can be physical or mental, concerned with posture or with thoughts. We may need confidence in ourselves, in the teaching, and in the teacher. Those who listen carefully to the instructions and follow them usually have the best results. Comparisons and inner arguments are not helpful. We need a trusting mind, such as children have who are eager to learn.

In order to meditate well, one has to be comfortable in body and mind. One of the preconditions for mental ease is joy. When one sits down to meditate, one truly wants to become still and quiet, without tensions in body or mind. Rigidity of the body is detrimental to expansion of the mind.

While concentration cannot yet be sustained, we must use all that arises to gain insight into ourselves, because greater insight also produces greater calm. The potential of the mind for concentrated one-pointedness exceeds any other mental capability. We can design a rocket to go to the moon and make it work very well, and still be extremely unhappy. The ability to concentrate the mind and to be one-pointed brings that inner poise which is not disturbed by external conditions. In the meditative practice, poise arises from inner happiness; a person who is unhappy cannot remain within, but will look for outside stimuli.

Questions

STUDENT: *Is there any difference in method between the first and second factor of absorption?*

AYYA KHEMA: First comes initial application and then sustained application. Determination and being comfortable with oneself are preconditions. It helps to recognize that meditative concentration is the epitome of human endeavor, and that everything else pales in comparison. The method of watching the breath does not change.

S: *Is it a sort of organic condition between the two factors?*

AK: Yes. All five factors follow each other organically and integrate with each other.

S: *Rather than switching techniques?*

AK: That's right.

S: *When I was in Thailand, I managed to reach the first meditative absorption. I had a feeling that my body wasn't mine any more, that I just had to take care of it as another living thing. I didn't feel ownership, just responsibility.*

AK: But that was after you came out of the absorption, not during it?

S: *Yes. Is that common?*

AK: It was a very important insight.

S: *I was frightened by it all. I had the feeling that something that had shown me great happiness was also going to show me the opposite, and I felt death coming. I realize now that it was the death of the ego that was actually coming.*

AK: Were you able at that time to discuss this with a teacher? No? That's a great pity. Was it long ago?

S: *It was nineteen years ago.*

AK: Nineteen! Can you remember anything that you did to get into the meditative absorption, and could you do it again?

S: *Yes, I remember. I would have to shut myself in a house for a week and try every method.*

AK: It doesn't have to be that drastic.

S: *I don't actually remember how I got to that point. The experience itself is the clearest experience of my whole life—as if it had happened yesterday. I have never been able to repeat this.*

AK: You didn't have the necessary guidance at the time. Once having done it, there will be off and on moments, but you can do it again. Can you remember any little thing that helped you?

S: *After I felt that I had voided my body and my mind so that I was empty, I took a mirror and looked the "I" in the eye, and all at once I knew there wasn't anybody there.*

AK: After you looked into the mirror, you were able to do the meditation?

S: *I sat outside and was sort of humming in unison with nature, and it was the first time in my life I had ever felt harmonious. There was no longer a sense of desperation and chronic disappointment.*

AK: How about this experience of looking in a mirror and seeing that there is actually nothing but the eye looking? Repeat something like that, and then sit down with the feeling of "There's nothing to worry about, let me just get on with it," and see if that helps. You can even bring the mirror in here. There is nothing to be scared of. Terror of appearances is one of the stages of insight. Terror of all that exists is a later insight.

The meditative absorptions are not unusual or so difficult that they are beyond our reach. The mind has a natural yearning for the peace they can provide.

S: *Can you do* vipassanā *while concentrating on the breath?*

AK: There are hardly any meditation methods that do not have the possibility of tranquility and insight, *samatha* and *vipassanā*. A method is a method by any name, and they are designed to complement each other.

S: *Do I know when I am doing* vipassanā *on the breath, as opposed to* samatha?

AK: When you are labeling your distracting thoughts, you are gaining insight into your own thinking pattern and procedure. You're also seeing the impermanence, the arising and ceasing of these thoughts, that there is nothing you can hang on to. There is absolutely no stability in them. If you put your attention on the fact that the breath is impermanent, and that its continuity hides its impermanence, that's insight.

If you can stay with the breath and sustain application, you are working toward calm. We use both directions because most people are unable, in the initial stages of meditation, to gain real calm or real insight. A little calm brings a little insight, and vice versa. So we always work on both levels, and eventually both come to fruition. Calm is the means, insight is the goal.

❧10 A Technique of Meditation

Now we are going to take a slightly different approach to the "sweeping" method of meditation. The results, too, can be different, and we shall discuss that later. First, concentrate on the breath, becoming aware of the feeling at the nostrils. Stay with that for a few moments.

Now transfer your full attention to the top of the head, to an area the size of a large coin. Become aware of any sensation, any feeling in that small area: pressure, warmth, pounding, movement, stillness, hardness, softness, contraction—any of those sensations, or any other. Then use your mind like a slowly opening fan, starting at the top of the head, slowly covering the top of the skull until you reach the crown of the head. Become aware of each particular spot until you have that whole area in your awareness, knowing sensations, knowing the feelings. It may be on the skin or under the skin, deeply within or on the surface. It may be sensations or emotions. Whatever you notice, know it fully, area after area, until the whole of the top of the skull is within your awareness.

Fix your attention on the crown of the head, on an area the size of a large coin. Try to penetrate into the feelings, the sensations, becoming one with that area. Then use your mind like a slowly opening fan. Starting at the crown of the head, gently move down the back of the head until you reach the base of the skull, becoming aware of each region, until the whole area is in your awareness.

Now move your attention to the left side of the head. Gently open up the awareness from the top of the skull, down the left side of the head, as far as the jaw line; from the hairline in front to behind the left ear, use your mind like a slowly opening fan, knowing each area and then keeping the whole area in your awareness. Know the feelings, the sensations. Be totally one-pointed, becoming one with the sensations or feelings.

Now transfer your attention to the right side of the head. Starting with the top of the skull, gently open up like a slowly opening fan, down the right side of the head to the jaw line, from the hairline in front to behind the right ear. Know each spot, and then be aware of the whole of that area.

Now try to become aware of the top of the head, the back of the head, and the right and left sides simultaneously, or as much of the head as you can.

Starting at the hairline above the forehead, gently open up your awareness down the whole of the face, as far as the chin and the jaw line, becoming aware of each region, until the whole area of the face is in your awareness. Know the feeling; know the sensation.

Try to become aware of the whole of the head, including the face, or as much of it as possible.

Now put your attention on the throat and the back of the neck simultaneously, or one after the other, holding on to the awareness of both. Gently open up from the jaw line and from the base of the skull, down the throat, down the back of the neck, to where they join the trunk, knowing each area, then knowing the whole. Be aware of the areas simultaneously, or one after the other, then hold on to the awareness of both.

Now concentrate on the left shoulder. Starting at the neck, gently open up the awareness like a slowly opening fan along the top of the left shoulder to where the arm joins, knowing each section and then knowing the whole, knowing the sensation, knowing feeling. Tickling, tingling, heaviness, lightness, worry, fear, transparency, movement, stillness—whatever may arise. Start at the left shoulder at the top of the left arm and gently open up your awareness down to the left elbow; open up like a slowly opening fan, all around the left upper arm. Know each area, then know the whole. Be one-pointed, try to be one with the area, with the sensation.

Starting at the left elbow, gently open up your awareness like a slowly open-ing fan, down the left lower arm to the wrist, all around, knowing each section and then knowing the whole area.

Now become aware of the left shoulder and the whole of the left arm as far as the wrist, or as much of these as possible, from the neck to the wrist.

Now become aware of the back and the palm of the left hand, either simul-taneously or one after the other, holding on to the awareness of both.

Fix your attention at the base of the five fingers of the left hand. Slowly move along the fingers to their tips. Keep your attention on the five tips, and make a mind movement out from the tips into the room.

Put your attention on the right shoulder. Starting at the neck, gradually open up awareness like a slowly opening fan to cover the whole of the right shoulder to where the arm joins. Know each section and then know the whole, one-pointedly becoming one with the area, and then with the sensation or the feeling.

Start at the top of the right upper arm. Slowly open up your awareness as far as the right elbow; know the sensation, know the feeling. First be aware of each section, then the whole.

Start at the right elbow. Gently open up the awareness, down the right lower arm as far as the wrist, all around, section after section, then know the whole, awareness and sensation being one.

Now become aware of the right shoulder and the whole of the right arm as far as the wrist, or as much of that as possible, from the neck to the wrist. Concentrate on the back and the palm of the right hand, simultaneously or one after the other, holding on to awareness of both.

Move your attention to the base of the five fingers of the right hand. Slowly move along the fingers to their tips. Keep your attention on the five tips, and make a mind movement out from the tips into the room.

Turn your attention to the front of the trunk. Starting at the shoulders, gently open up your awareness like a slowly opening fan as far as the waist, becoming aware of each section, and then knowing the whole of the area, knowing the sensation, the feeling. Tingly, light, painful, pleasant, warm, solid, transparent—any of these, or any others.

Starting at the waist in front, gently open up your awareness down the lower part of the trunk to the groin, knowing each area, and then being aware of the whole, becoming one with the sensation, with the feeling, being one-pointed.

Put your attention on the whole of the front of the trunk, from the shoulders to the groin, all at once, or taking in as much of it as possible. Know the feeling, know the sensation.

Now move your attention to the back. Starting at the shoulders, gently open up the awareness as far as the waist. Become aware of each area, and then know the whole.

Starting at the waist at the back, gently open up your awareness down to the buttocks, as far as where the legs join; know each area, then know the whole.

Now become aware of the whole of the back, starting from the shoulders to where the legs join, or as much of all that as possible.

Become aware of the whole of the trunk, from shoulders to groin, from shoulders to buttocks, front and back, complete as a whole, or as much of it as you can. Know the sensation, know the feeling.

Now include both arms with the front and the back of the trunk.

Place your attention on the left thigh. Starting from the groin, gently open up your awareness as far as the left knee, knowing area after area until the whole of the left thigh comes into your awareness.

Starting at the left knee, gently open up your awareness down the left lower leg as far as the ankle, section by section, until the whole area comes within your attention. Know the feelings and the sensations one-pointedly.

Now become aware of the whole of the left leg from the groin to the ankle, or as much of that as possible.

Move your attention to the sole and the upper part of the left foot, simultaneously or one after the other, holding on to the awareness of both.

Fix your attention on the base of the five toes of the left foot; slowly move along the toes to their tips. Put your full attention on the five tips, and make a mind movement out from the tips into the room.

Move your attention to the right thigh. Starting at the groin, gently open up your awareness, down and around the right thigh as far as the right knee; know each area and then know the whole, one-pointedly, at one with the sensation.

Starting at the right knee, gently open up your awareness, down the right lower leg as far as the ankle, becoming aware of each section, and then knowing the whole.

Become aware of the whole of the right leg from groin to ankle, or as much of the area as possible.

Put your attention on the sole and the top of the right foot, simultaneously or one after the other, holding on to the awareness of both, knowing the sensation.

Turn your attention to the base of the five toes of the right foot. Slowly move along the toes to their tips. Keep your attention on the five tips, and make a mind movement out from the tips into the room.

Now become aware of both legs from groin to ankle, simultaneously or one after the other, holding on to awareness of both.

Concentrate on the soles and the tops of both feet, simultaneously or one after the other, holding on to awareness of both, becoming one with the sensation.

Move your attention to the base of all ten toes. Slowly move along the toes to their tips.

Put your attention on the ten tips, and make a mind movement out from the tips into the room.

Now come back to the whole of your body and try to become aware from the top of the head to the tips of the toes, or as much of the whole as possible, including as many areas as you can. Become one with the sensation, awareness and sensation being one.

Place your attention at the base of the ten toes. Slowly move along the toes to the tips. Put your attention on the ten tips, and make a mind movement out into the room.

The first method was called "part by part." This one is called "full sweep." Each serves a different function. The first is geared to gaining insight, to becoming aware of one's reactions, to the recognition of impermanence and corelessness. This second method is directed toward calm. It doesn't work for everybody, but it is designed for that purpose. It often serves as an entry into meditative absorptions.

Whoever was able to have pleasant feelings in the body can use these feelings as the subject of meditation. One doesn't necessarily have to go through the whole of the body as we have just done, but the moment the pleasant feeling arises in the body, these sensations become the subject of meditation. That constitutes the initial step toward the first meditative absorption, being one aspect of it. It is, of course, much easier to become absorbed in something pleasant than in a rather neutral feeling, so this enables a meditator to bring sustained application to the subject of meditation. Then all five factors of the first meditative absorption become possible.

It doesn't matter whether the whole body or just parts of it are filled with the pleasant feeling, because it is the sensation that matters as the subject of meditation. When it is absolutely clear that this kind of sensation is something you want to keep your attention on, then it will lead into the first absorption. It is one of the methods available, one of the keys to open the door. This method doesn't open the door for everyone, but it certainly does, in a fairly simple way, for quite a few people.

If the pleasant feeling arises before you have gone even halfway through the body, that's fine. There is no need to continue the "sweeping," but instead use the feeling as the subject of meditation.

QUESTIONS

STUDENT: *What part does visualization play in this?*

AYYA KHEMA: It plays a part only if you have to use it to arouse feelings. Visualization is not part of this method. This is the second foundation of mindfulness, which is strictly concerned with feelings. If feelings only arise when you visualize the part of the body you are concentrating on, then just remember that visualization itself is not enough; feelings are the primary object.

S: *I found myself being able to feel the various parts, but then I tended to visualize them too. Sometimes I came to a part that was irritated or painful. I was sort of looking right into the middle of the dark. I wasn't trying to do that, but it kept happening anyway.*

AK: As long as you have feelings, then the visualization is fine.

S: *Are you saying that visualization will help to get to the feeling?*

AK: Some people need to visualize. It is not part of the practice, but sometimes it is necessary as a crutch. If so, one must not leave it at the visual stage, but attend to feelings and sensations.

S: *I kind of felt the body looking at the body.*

AK: The body cannot look at the body.

S: *The mind is a part of the body, and it was looking at the body, and there was another that was looking at both of them.*

AK: The mind was looking at the body, and the mind was watching the mind...that's quite possible, but it is not the aim of meditation and doesn't lead to calm or insight.

S: *When I do this practice, I am concerned that I cover all the body parts. Would you say that that is not so important?*

AK: To be perfect is the prerogative of the enlightened. Let's just relax and do the best we can. Whatever part you miss on one occasion, you will cover the next time.

S: *If I am using this method daily, do I do it once or twice?*

AK: You can do "part by part" once a day and the "full sweep" also once a day. You can use a little imagination, and practice in whatever way works best for you. Some people combine the two methods.

LOVING-KINDNESS MEDITATION

Before starting, concentrate on the breath for just a moment.

Think of yourself as your own mother and your own child. We all have a child within us and also a mother. Think of yourself as the mother who loves her child with all its faults and all its difficulties; the mother who loves and protects, cares, and who with wisdom shows the right way. Look at yourself in that way. Embrace yourself with motherly love.

Think of the person sitting nearest you as if he or she were your own child. Extend the love of a mother to that person with care and concern, and embrace that person with motherly love.

Extend that same love to everyone present. Imagine they are all your children and you care deeply for them, are truly concerned. You wish to help them grow. Embrace everyone with motherly love.

Now think of your parents as if they were your children, reversing the roles. You are the mother; love them with all their difficulties, help them, care for them.

Think of those people who are nearest and dearest to you as your children. Fill them with your love, with your care and concern, and embrace them with this total love.

Think of your friends as being your children, so that you can fill them and surround them with the love of a mother, caring and concerned, wishing to help.

Think of anyone whom you find difficult to love, and consider that person as your own child. Children are often difficult. Think of yourself as the mother of that person, and see how the difficulties become negligible, or even dissolve. Extend your love and your compassion to that person, embracing him or her with your motherly love.

Think of people you meet in daily life—in the shops, on the street, while traveling. Think of them as your children, and extend the same motherly love to all of them, opening up your heart so that it may become wide and accepting, so spacious that there is room for all these people.

Now open up your heart even wider, as wide as possible—without barriers, without limits—and let this motherly love flow out from it to as many beings as possible, near and far, embracing all of them, filling them with your care and concern, wishing to help, hoping for their wellbeing.

Turn your attention back to yourself. Embrace yourself as your own mother. Accept all the existing childish difficulties with a loving heart, with a smile, and fill yourself from head to toe with the joy and contentment that arise from loving and giving.

May all beings feel love in their hearts.

11 Further Steps

STEPS 5–7

IN THE DISCOURSE on transcendental dependent arising, the next, deeper absorptions now follow. Having entered the first room of the eight-room mansion mentioned earlier, there is no real difficulty in making our way into the other rooms. It is a natural progression.

In the second absorption two factors disappear: initial application and sustained application. They are no longer necessary, because if one has been able to concentrate one-pointedly, there is no need to apply oneself again. So it is a natural progression that centers upon one of the factors that arose in the first meditative absorption, namely, happiness, inner joy. Because of the very pleasant physical sensations that are present in the first absorption, joy arises. In the second absorption one has to separate the physical feeling from emotional joy. The meditator now knows quite consciously that physical feelings are still very gross sensations, and naturally wants to progress toward something more subtle. Emotional joy is comparatively more subtle than pleasant physical feelings. Since joy is already present in the first absorption, there is no difficulty in focusing on it. It's a matter of separation, which means letting go of the physical sensation and fixing one's attention on the emotional aspect of being happy.

It is a progressive letting go, and the first step is to let go of the pleasant physical sensation. Both the physical feeling and the joy are somewhat akin to exhilaration. They are, at first, quite amazing and exciting. Although they demand some depth of concentration, there is a natural recognition that this surely cannot be all.

In the second meditative absorption, self-confidence arises. This is not a feeling of superiority, which is usually based on a feeling of inferiority, but the certainty of being able to find happiness within, and at will. When the process is still "hit or miss," it does not inspire confidence; however, when it becomes an established procedure, self-confidence is gained. This self-confidence is not only based on finding happiness within but also on the ability to make progress on the spiritual path—a progress so marked that one knows with certainty that it is entirely different from one's former discursive thinking, so that an inner stability is created. This self-confidence in one's ability to proceed on the spiritual path and to find happiness within bears fruit in our daily life. One outcome, which is quite significant, is a lessening of the need for appreciation and support from others, because with inner support, one is moving toward independence and self-sufficiency.

Since we are all looking for happiness, to be self-sufficient in happiness is, of course, a very important step. Up to that point we have been looking for happiness somewhere outside ourselves. To become really self-sufficient in our most significant emotional aspect carries with it an inner security, which is not dependent on other people's approval. Neither does it depend on the understanding or the love of others. If these are not available, happiness is not in any way impaired.

Inner happiness depends on concentration and not on someone else's approval. From that realization arises a very distinct understanding that one is the maker of one's own happiness or unhappiness. One loses a lot of the foolishness that most of us carry around, namely thinking thoughts detrimental to our own happiness. The practice of tranquility, if carried out correctly, brings insight, and is the skillful means toward that end.

Insights arise to an intelligent mind as an inner reality. There is nothing to grasp or crave in order to gain insight. Understanding our experience makes it possible to relate cause to effect and be deeply touched. This applies to all experiences in our life. Not watching carefully when crossing a street and almost being run over enables us to relate crossing the street to being more careful, without searching for that insight. It's an automatic progression. Having experienced inner happiness that results from concentration, we automatically realize that other people or outside circumstances do not of themselves make us happy or unhappy. It's entirely up to us. The arising of self-confidence shows us that we are actually capable of making ourselves happy, not through indulgence or through pleasures of the senses, but strictly through spiritual practice. Self-discipline is the most important, most significant aspect of staying with the practice and gradually acknowledging its priority more and more.

Although the second meditative absorption brings self-confidence, the meditator knows that its inherent experience of inner joy still has a certain gross aspect, because it contains a subtle excitement. As a natural further progression, he or she inclines toward something more restful, more peaceful.

The next depth of absorption can be described as contentment. Traditionally it is not called by that name, but in experiencing it, that quality is evidenced. The mind is settling down, whereas at the stages of physical rapture and inner joy it appears to be flying high. The actual experience feels as if the mind is moving into a new depth. Wishes and desires that are usually present, even subconsciously, subside after we have experienced inner joy. When there is no desire, no craving, then there is also no suffering, and that brings peaceful contentment.

An interesting analogy is used in one of the commentaries on the first four absorptions, which vividly illustrates what happens.

A person is wandering through the desert without any water and is suffering from extreme thirst. This is us when we are beset by discursive thoughts. We are thirsting for peacefulness, inner ease, and harmony while wandering through the desert of our discursive thinking. No relief is yet in sight.

The wanderer in the desert sees a pool of water in the distance. He becomes quite excited and certainly extremely interested. This relates to the first absorption, containing physical rapture, which has an element of excitement in it. It is possible to translate the word *pīti* (physical rapture) as "interest," because usually real interest in meditation begins at this point—a feeling of hopefulness and pleasure arises that relief from thirst is near.

The wanderer draws close to the water, stands right at the edge of it, and knows he will now be able to find relief. There is happiness mingled with excitement at this prospect. This is an analogy for the second meditative absorption. He bends down to drink and is content, having obtained what he needed and wanted. Finally, he lies down in the shade of a nearby tree, totally at ease.

The third meditative absorption is described as contentment, the physical feeling of rapture having disappeared. One-pointedness and happiness are the two factors remaining of the five initial aspects encountered in the first absorption. In the fourth absorption, only one-pointedness remains; this results in equanimity, or total peacefulness, comparable to our wanderer having found complete ease in the shade of a tree. This peacefulness is of such depth that sounds are no longer heard, and it is a complete rest for the mind. This is the state of meditation in which the mind recharges itself with new energy.

We are apt to take the mind for granted. It thinks from morning to night and it dreams from night to morning, constantly busy. We expect that it will keep on doing that, and we hope that one day it may do it better. Unless we provide an opportunity for it to do so, it is highly unlikely that it will. On the contrary, it will do it increasingly badly, because the mind, being the finest tool in the whole universe, has to be treated like any other delicate tool. If it is abused and not given a moment's rest, it will eventually stop functioning, or at least it will not function very well. So instead of hoping that our mind will one day do better, we should realize that by overworking it with all our discursive thinking we shall blunt its capacity. The mind has the potential to regenerate itself, and it is imperative that we make use of that potential. When the mind is totally at rest, when it does not have to attend to any sense contacts, it is completely secluded, and can revert back to its primal purity to regenerate its energy.

The four absorptions are modes of getting in touch with the original purity of the mind, which is available when we are not thinking. It is our thinking process that brings the defilements or impurities. We have lost the ability to stop thinking, and therefore we are no longer aware of the original purity. In the meditative absorptions we have an opportunity to retrieve the original mind, which has the potential for rapture, joy, contentment, and peace. Our experience of these states makes it possible to progress on the path of insight.

When we experience deep peace and contentment, with no wishes, no problems, the world can no longer hold the same attraction for us as it used to, and we have taken a step toward liberation. When we have the ability to actualize within ourselves exactly that which we have subconsciously yearned for, then we will no longer search for happiness outside.

The experience of a totally peaceful state of mind, which has no contact with the senses, tells us that our senses are our temptations. They are constantly tempting us into reacting. Only when we have had an experience without sense contacts—so much superior in happiness to anything we have previously known—are we willing and able to abandon our search for pleasant feelings. This doesn't mean that we shall be without agreeable sensations from now on; but our expectation that we shall find fulfillment through our senses is dropped, and with it all disappointments. When we no longer look for lasting results through our senses, we are able to enjoy ourselves far more fully.

As a result of the peacefulness of the meditative absorptions, the mind gains the ability to accept the premise of no individual personality. The mind that does not possess its own inner happiness and peace finds it hard to accept that all our striving has been in vain. But the mind that is already peaceful and happy has no objection. On the contrary, it is delighted to find that worldly matters are truly inferior. The path through the meditative absorptions to insight is beset with far fewer obstacles to the acceptance of absolute reality.

Although it is possible to gain insight without the meditative absorptions, because the mind calms down anyway when meditation is practiced for long enough, it is a difficult path. The mind revolts against the unknown and untried, and it very often blocks off the insights, which a completely happy, contented, and peaceful mind would never do. On the contrary, a contented mind is wide open, pliable, malleable, and expansive. The Buddha took the path of the meditative absorptions.

Some people are more inclined toward the peaceful, calm, and gentle way, and others are attracted to a dynamic, quick, and forceful approach. The latter easily results in resistance. It is to our advantage to use the absorption capacity of our mind to alter our level of awareness to the point where we have no difficulty in accepting the absolute truth of "being nobody." That takes courage and a willingness to relinquish our concepts. To meditate without discursive thinking requires the abandonment of our ego awareness, which only exists through the support of our thoughts. Naturally, the ego manifests itself again after we come out of meditation. But if we have had the blissful experience of no "I," even momentarily, we will find it much easier to recognize the ego illusion.

The first three meditative absorptions are not difficult to achieve. It is a matter of relaxing, letting go, with no desire to be anything or anyone or to gain new knowledge. We allow the mind to settle down, to release itself from conceptual thinking, from its worries and ideas, and to concentrate on the subject of meditation instead. People often find it difficult even to form an idea of inner joy, much less experience it. We need to accept the fact that it exists within us and that we can discover it.

Meditative absorptions are dependent on inner purity, even though that purity may be momentary. Whatever purity we can arouse in daily living helps us to enter into the meditative absorptions. To attain purity in daily living means that we are mindful of our thoughts and our reactions, so that we can let go of unwholesome and negative ones. This makes the meditative path much easier. The way of practice with the meditative absorptions creates a deep-seated interest and keeps us on the meditation pillow, which in turn makes daily life far easier to cope with. It is no longer full of great burdens and difficulties, but only contains the ordinary unsatisfactoriness that is universally acceptable, and doesn't impinge on one's consciousness in such a way that one feels depressed or unhappy about it. Although we can't carry our meditation experience with us into daily life, we certainly carry a residue that sustains us, and the mind knows it has a home to which it can retreat.

Questions

STUDENT: *Is it possible to practice both calm and insight at the same time?*

AYYA KHEMA: When it is possible for the mind to enter into the absorptions, insights are generated spontaneously. Both have to be practiced.

S: *Does discursive thinking totally disappear, or does it just lose its solidity?*

AK: In the beginning it loses its solidity; that is called "neighborhood concentration"—when we need no longer put a label on our thoughts. Thinking becomes like a cloud in the background. The next step is to lose even that wispy kind of thinking and be only with the breath. The mind eventually relaxes and is absorbed in the breath, so that mind and breath become one.

S: *You said at one point that terror arises when we realize that we are not the personality we thought we were. Could that be the first real experience of "egolessness"?*

AK: It is a result of experiencing impermanence so strongly that we find nothing to hang on to. Then there is "nobody," but because this terrifies us, it cannot develop into a path moment of total inner vision.

S: *Do we automatically develop a happy mind as we progress through the absorptions, or do we have to make a special effort, such as practicing more loving-kindness meditations?*

AK: For some people, loving-kindness meditations can in themselves be an entry into absorptions. When we are able to open our hearts, our minds do the same.

S: *Would these absorptions happen in one meditation session, or is this something that takes many years? Does one finish with one absorption and stop a while before going on to the next?*

AK: They follow each other quickly if there's some guidance. The first and second absorptions actually arise together—we just have to differentiate between them—and the third is a natural progression. The fourth is more difficult; more time has to be spent in meditation, such as is available in a solitary retreat, for instance.

S: *Can one do this without a teacher?*

AK: Yes, but it's tedious, it takes much longer, and it isn't quite as satisfying, because one is never quite sure that one is doing it correctly. In the end one usually looks for somebody to substantiate one's own experiences.

$\lessapprox$12 Nonmaterial Meditative Absorptions

USUALLY WHEN WE HAVE AN EXPERIENCE, we also have an inner observer—the one who knows. The observer is still part of our ego concept. To enter into deeper states of concentration, it is necessary to have the experience of the fourth fine-material absorption. The mind can expand from there to a level of consciousness called "the base of infinite space." Initially we have a sense of the body being so enlarged that it loses itself in infinity. A gradual or an immediate expansion are both possibilities, but the result is the same. The awareness is of a spatial sense of infinity in which no personal body, or other bodies, are discernible.

The correlation between the first of the nonmaterial absorptions and the first of the fine-material absorptions concerns experiences arising from the body. One of these involves pleasant sensations, and here it relates to expansion. Only two things exist in the universe with which we should concern ourselves: mind and matter. And so in meditation it also has to be either the one or the other. Although these experiences arise from the body (matter), they happen in a totally different manner from the ones we are used to. We are used to looking after our body, dealing with its many aches and pains, its desires and needs. In deep meditation we are faced with the loss of individual body awareness.

Insight arises from the feeling that infinity is a primordial ocean, out of which untold numbers of little bubbles arise. In due course these little bubbles disappear into the ocean again. While they are on the surface they become aware of themselves as individuals. They completely forget that they arose out of an infinite ocean and will sink back into it again; they believe themselves, in their brief emergence, to be beautiful, clever, stupid, better, or worse than other bubbles. One bubble might say to another bubble, "Look at me, I'm so big." And the other may reply, "Look at me, I'm so pretty." In reality they are both simply bubbles rising out of the endless ocean to which they will quickly return, as bubbles always do.

In this infinity of space, nothing can be found but space. The realization emerges that the belief in a personal body and other individual bodies (human or otherwise), trees, flowers, or rocks is nothing but an illusion. Our belief that each bubble is a separate entity is shaken. Having experienced a space in which nothing can be found, especially no "me," we automatically realize that a totality exists that has no separations. Out of that totality, manifestations arise and disappear again.

The next step in meditative absorptions is called "infinity of consciousness." Again, we find a correlation with the second meditative absorption in the fine-material sphere, in which the physical factor of the sensation is transformed into the emotions of joy and happiness. Here, we move from the physical aspect of complete expansion to the mental aspect of infinity of consciousness, in which there is no personal consciousness to be found. Both the physical and mental aspects arise simultaneously, just as they do in the first and second meditative absorption, where joy comes simultaneously with pleasant feelings, since it is impossible not to be joyous when pleasant feelings are present. By the same token, it is impossible to be aware of infinity of space without infinity of consciousness. Both must arise together. In order to take the next step, one has to turn one's attention away from one and direct it to the other.

This in itself is an important facet of the practice that leads to liberation: to turn one's attention away from worldly matters toward that which is the unconditioned, the liberating freedom. Both are available in our consciousness. As we learn to do that in meditation—to turn away from that which is impending, destroying, and disturbing, and toward that which is peaceful and wholesome—we learn to alter our focus of attention. We need not continue to be attentive to that which brings only worldly results.

The infinity of consciousness gives rise to the realization that no personal consciousness exists. There is nobody with a separate mind and body; just bubbles arising out of "craving to be" and disappearing again.

Consciousness expansion sometimes seems to begin from the limits of one's own mind, which gradually loses its boundaries. Infinity of consciousness is an experience during which we are not burdened with the ego concept, and therefore we do not have to be, to achieve, to do, to know, to become. All the pressures on us disappear at that time completely. The expansion of consciousness leaves no room for any personal concept, idea, or desire. There is only awareness, but it is not "mine."

The next step in this progression is also a very natural one, similar to the correlation to the fine-material absorptions where, following upon the experience of joy, one is naturally contented. In the nonmaterial absorptions we now enter into the "base of nothingness." Nothingness is often misunderstood; to illustrate it, the following analogy could be useful: when we come into the meditation room, we see a lot of cushions, people, and decorations on the shrine. Then someone comes along and clears the whole place out. When we come in again we find nothing, only empty space. The room has been completely emptied. But that doesn't mean we recognize nothing, only that we realize that there is nothing there.

To reach the base of nothingness is a natural progression from our experience of infinite consciousness. We realize that this spaciousness we are experiencing, this ultimate consciousness, is empty of any phenomena. There is nothing there that we can hold on to, that can give us security; we can't grab a star and say, "This one is mine," and keep it as our resting place. There is absolute emptiness in this meditation experience. In it we find a totality of existence in which nothing particular is to be found of which we could say, "It's me, it's mine, I want it, I'll have it, I'll keep it." The analogy of the emptied room may give some idea of this particular experience. Eventually, one has to bite into a mango to know the taste of it. These three nonmaterial absorptions are natural progressions, and once the mind has become sufficiently concentrated, they follow one another fairly easily.

The next step, the eighth absorption, is more difficult; just like the fourth of the fine-material absorptions. It is called "neither perception nor nonperception." The mind ceases to perceive even peacefulness but remains awake and alert. It is a state in which the peacefulness of the fourth absorption is surpassed, because then there was still the perception of peace. Now even that has been suspended. One could literally say that it is a state of suspension and therefore the most energizing condition for the mind. The difficulty inherent in both—the fourth and the eighth step—is that one has to give oneself up; the same difficulty one encounters when practicing for liberation. These meditative states are therefore excellent preconditions for the final letting go. To use a metaphor, one must, in a sense, be willing to drown. One has to give oneself up completely and let go of all preconceived notions of what one is, will be, or could be. The ability to let go even for a moment is part of the necessary training on the path to liberation. Although in all the absorptions there is still someone who is experiencing them, this is so minute an element that a glimpse into emptiness may be possible.

When the Buddha practiced the meditative absorptions, he realized that unsatisfactoriness and ego were in evidence once again when meditation ended. He knew there was something more to be done. This was his great contribution and innovation to the meditative path, which had itself already been in existence for about two and a half thousand years. Having come to the experience of "neither perception nor nonperception," it is easy to imagine that one has reached such a high state of purification and realization that nothing else needs to be done. But that is a misconception, and the Buddha's own example points to the absorptions as a means toward insight—wisdom.

In order to practice, we must make a resolution: "I will not be deterred from my subject of meditation, I will stay with it! Every time I wander off, I'll be back!" In other words, we must use the will to counteract the discursive tendency of the mind. Then we need to drop that determination, to leave the mind free to concentrate. Our next step is to arouse a feeling of contentment and happiness about ourselves and then to keep the mind tethered, not allowing it to play its usual games. Once it has learned to obey, it will stay like that naturally. The mind doesn't actually enjoy these thinking games; it feels bothered by them and experiences unsatisfactoriness. The mind is far happier if it can remain one-pointed, because even a short period of one-pointedness brings some peacefulness. The feeling of peacefulness may be cultivated by keeping one's attention on it for as long as possible.

An easy entry into the first absorption is the technique we have just practiced: to make awareness of pleasant sensations one's focus of attention when the whole body becomes involved with them. Loving-kindness meditation is another possible entry, in which we use the spiritual heart center, considered to be in the middle of the chest, and feel the warmth emanating from it. By opening the heart we increase the blissful sensation, which can be used for entry into the absorptions.

The absorptions constitute the pleasure path of practice. The Buddha said, "This is a pleasure I allow myself." The absorptions keep us in a balanced state between the self-discipline needed for practice and that needed for its enjoyment. Hoping, wishing, and expecting are all detrimental to concentration. We can only do one thing at a time; we can either hope and expect, or we can concentrate. If we leave the mind alone and actually allow it to settle into and become one with the subject of meditation, it will concentrate of its own accord. That ability is a natural quality of the mind. It is a letting go of all our preconceived notions, ideas, beliefs, and viewpoints. The more we can let go, the easier life becomes. The same applies to the meditative absorptions. The more we can let go of what we have heard, believed, and hoped for, and just sit down and pay attention, the easier the meditation. All views and ideas are detrimental to actual practice. We can pick our views and ideas up again when we leave our meditation, and we can carry them around with us again if we want to. They are nothing but a burden. If we were to let go, we would find the truth within.

One of the qualities of an enlightened one is that he has no views. Having experienced the truth, there is no view. One description of an enlightened one (found in the *Mangala Sutta*) is that "although touched by worldly circumstance, his mind never wavers. Stainless, sorrowless, and secure, his is the highest blessing." Every time we detect habitual viewpoints it is very helpful to drop them, at least for the period of the meditation. Only then will the meditation flourish.

If we take a little time to consider whether everything that is so important to us is, in an absolute sense, really essential, we may find that we can just as easily let go. When we look after our own spiritual and emotional growth, everything and everyone we touch benefits.

QUESTIONS

STUDENT: *Referring to the meditative absorptions, do you then perceive reality in a different way and practice with that as motivation?*

AYYA KHEMA: Certainly the motivation becomes automatic. Having experienced something that gives far greater happiness than anything else we have ever known, nobody has to be urged to sit down and meditate.

S: *I am curious to know how much emphasis to place on nonclinging to even the best experience.*

AK: If you cling to experiences, they lose their value and become "imperfections of insight." We are always willing to experience the impermanence of our suffering, but here we must be prepared to experience the impermanence of our pleasure. This can be quite a penetrating experience because we can actually watch the dissolution of the pleasant states. Because meditators may cling to such pleasant meditative states, they are considered to constitute the wrong path. The Buddha taught the absorptions and clearly gave instructions not to cling to them, because nonclinging is synonymous with liberation.

S: *I think another reason why teachers do not teach the meditative absorptions is because it can produce dissatisfaction in the student who hasn't had such experiences.*

AK: That reaction is possible whatever meditation method is being taught. However, with guidance it is immeasurably easier to enter into the absorptions. There are always two directions on which to focus: insight and calm; both bring satisfying results. Many people unwittingly enter into absorption states, and without guidance they are unable to benefit from them sufficiently. Naturally, not getting what one wants results in suffering, but that can be used as a learning experience. Because of these various fears, we need a commonsense approach to meditation and an acceptance of the fact that the absorption states are factors of enlightenment.

S: *What happens when a practitioner has accomplished the first, second, and third meditative absorptions and at that point finds it impossible to move into the fourth one?*

AK: Even three absorption states give the mind a different base from which to operate. However, it is highly unlikely that a complete stand-still should take place; time, patience, and determination overcome such obstacles.

S: *What does it mean, to "carry on"?*

AK: Even the first three meditative absorptions greatly facilitate insight and give the spiritual path the needed impetus, so we can continue without wavering. They give the mind its natural home, and as we continue to practice, they provide an understood experience that makes higher states of consciousness accessible.

LOVING-KINDNESS MEDITATION

Please focus your attention on the breath for just a moment.

Imagine that your heart contains nothing but golden light and that this golden light fills you from head to toe with its golden gleam, with its warmth, bringing you contentment and joy. This golden light surrounds you, so that you can sit in it and feel at ease and contented.

Now let the golden light from your heart go out to the person sitting nearest you and fill him or her with its golden gleam, with its warmth, contentment, and joy. Surround that person with golden light, giving him or her a feeling of safety and security.

Let that golden light from your heart grow so that it reaches out to every-one sitting with you, filling them with the warmth from your heart, giving them a gift of joy and contentment, and surrounding them with the golden light of your love, your compassion.

Now let the golden light from your heart reach out to your parents, filling them with the warmth from your heart, giving them contentment and joy, surrounding them with your love, giving them a feeling of security.

Now think of those people who are nearest and dearest to you, and let that golden light from your heart reach out to them, filling them with it, surrounding them with it, bringing your love and warmth to them.

Think of all your friends. Let the golden light from your heart reach out to them, bringing them your friendship and your love, surrounding them with it, bringing them your gift of contentment, joy, and safety.

Think of all the people you have met, whether they are known to you or not. Let the golden light increase and spread out to all of them, filling them with your friendship and your love, and surrounding them with the warmth from your heart.

Now think of all the people who live near you, whether you have seen or met them or not.

Let the golden light from your heart grow until it reaches all of them, filling them with your warmth and your friendship, and surrounding them with the golden light, giving them love and safety.

Now let the golden light from your heart grow and expand until it is like a golden cloud over the whole of the country. Let the golden drops from this cloud fall into everyone's heart, bringing them warmth, contentment, and security.

Now put your attention back on yourself. Feel the warmth that comes from your heart surrounding you and filling you, bringing you contentment and joy.

May beings everywhere be joyful and contented.

✤13 Knowledge and Vision of Things as They Really Are

STEP 8

TRANSCENDENTAL DEPENDENT ARISING concerns causes and their effects. The next step that follows on from the meditative absorptions is called "the knowledge and vision of things as they really are" (*yathābhūtañāna-dassana*). Vision is the inner experience and knowledge is the understanding of it. The understood experience of "things as they are" means insight. From a practical standpoint, we first enter into the meditative absorptions and subsequently use the strength and calm of the mind to gain insight.

In the Buddha's terminology, insight means to understand through one's own experience the three characteristics of all that exists, namely impermanence, unsatisfactoriness, and corelessness. Impermanence is masked by continuity. Because the breath continues to arise, we forget that each breath is new, the old one discarded and useless. Unsatisfactoriness is masked by change, by movement. Sometimes we run away from it, distract ourselves, or move our body. Corelessness is masked by compactness, solidity. In order to see things as they really are, we must break down the obstacles, embedded in our concepts, that show us continuity as permanence, and compactness and solidity as self or substance. This is made more difficult by the fact that we dislike impermanence, unsatisfactoriness, and being without substance, because these can destroy our cherished ego concept.

The first step on the insight path is to delineate mind and matter. This means experiencing this person, "I," not as one compact whole, but as consisting of body and mind. In our meditative practice, breath is matter, and awareness of the breath is mind. When we focus on the breath and fail to concentrate sufficiently to experience serenity, we can at least recognize these two aspects, which is far more useful and profitable than our habitual discursive thinking. When we are fully aware of these two aspects, the compactness and solidity of the person, "I," begins to break down.

Mind and matter exist everywhere. It may not be the kind of mind that we ourselves have, but even a tree or any other natural phenomenon has craving for existence, otherwise it can't survive. When we become imbued with the understanding of mind and matter in ourselves, we will also see it in all that surrounds us. We can observe it internally and externally.

The Buddha said, "The whole of the universe, O monks, lies in this fathom-long body and mind." We start our observation of underlying reality with our subject of meditation and extend that understanding to all that enters our awareness. Mind and matter are interdependent but not identical. Unless we have this basic understanding of ourselves, we do not have the means to delve deeper into insight. We will be blocked by "Yes, but...," which is the expression of skeptical doubt. We need to understand that the mind is in charge and orders the body around. Even the breath, which is essential to life, can be given commands by the mind. We can tell it to stop a moment, or to deepen, or to slow down. Even though breathing is mostly an autonomous action of the body, it can still be changed by the mind.

Subsequently we realize that neither mind nor matter are solid units but instead consist of heaps, or movements. Each thought is a movement of impulses in the mind. The body only appears to be solid; with mindfulness we can feel that there is continuous movement. As we watch the breath intently and become concentrated, we notice that the breath actually contains movement within and is never one solid breath. It has a beginning, a middle, and an end, and fluctuates incessantly. As our own mental formations stand out more clearly, we notice their heap-like characteristics, which resemble electrical impulses. We gain a deeper understanding of the nature of the self that formerly seemed so compact and solid.

What appears solid to us is actually like the dust in the air that we can see when sunlight strikes it. The same applies to our bodies. Our experience and understanding of this fact enables us to gain a foothold in insight. Knowing about it and pondering it does not suffice. It is a beginning, but it has to become an understood experience. If understanding is lacking, the experience is in vain. Our watchfulness is also movement, just as we notice change and the lack of a solid core in feelings and sensations.

If these aspects are known experientially, not intellectually, we will see everything in a different light. We will get a feeling for the fact that only impermanent phenomena exist. We will lose some of our attachment to these phenomena. Solidity and continuity breed attachment. When we experience the opposite of these in our meditation, we open the way to true insight.

Now we come to an understanding of cause and condition, which means that we realize that all bodies, all matter, consist of the four primary elements. We can feel the temperature of heat or cold in the body, the wind of breath, the water in sweat or saliva, and the earth element in the solid bones and flesh of the body. We can realize that those elements are not self-sustaining or unconditioned but are dependent for their existence upon correlating factors. Because the elements are constantly changing in their consistency, our bodies, being dependent upon them, also change their consistency; therefore most of the time there is some discomfort. That can easily be experienced, and then insight into our body's pain arises.

Our mental awareness is also conditioned. When it arises as a thought process, it does so because of a sense contact. Our sense consciousness generates feeling, and perception and related thoughts follow. The functioning of our mind is dependent upon contact—seeing, hearing, touching, smelling, tasting, or ideation. When we watch in the meditative state the chain reaction of sense contact followed by feeling, then by perception or naming, then by the thought process (which is usually craving or rejection), we will know this as a reality and not just as a description. When there is pain and the mind reacts to it and wants to get rid of it, it is due to the touch contact that generates the unpleasant feeling. The mind explains it as pain and then reacts to it by disliking it, wanting to get away from it. If we observe this process in meditation, we can then see it in all our mind states, which in turn are based on an underlying condition, not self-sustaining, not independent. This gives rise to the understanding that there is nobody in charge. If there were a "self," surely that "self" would have enough sense to think only happy thoughts and have only pleasant feelings.

Observing pleasant or unpleasant feelings and our reactions to them helps us to realize the circumstances involved in creating "me." Knowing this clearly, we can make use of this understanding in daily life. We no longer have to believe what our mind concocts, but we realize it is caused by a condition, a trigger. It is up to us to turn the mind in wholesome directions.

Having realized these truths for ourselves, having deliberated on them and checked their veracity, we will then be able to concentrate on them far more effectively than ever before. These insights are a natural progression.

Because mind and matter arise due to causes, it follows that there are also causes and conditions for our birth, namely, craving and ignorance. Ignorance in this context means ignoring absolute truth, and craving here means "craving to be." These conditions must necessarily bring about defilements, resulting in unskillful actions. Even our skillful actions are based on our ego concept and therefore have effects. The understanding of causes and conditions needs to be extended further into our karmic results, which are not attributable to fate or accident, but are due to our own intentions. The Buddha's teaching is sometimes called the teaching of cause and effect. It is meant as a teaching of analysis, because in order to penetrate into a real understanding of ourselves as phenomena, we have to analyze. It is not just a matter of logical conclusions but rather of using inner vision, based on our own experience.

We now come to the most significant aspect of insight, namely, the examination of arising and ceasing, which is the quality of impermanence. What has arisen from certain causes and conditions must cease, because all causes and conditions also cease. When we realize that the in-breath has already stopped and another one has taken its place, and that one will also cease to make room for the next one, we get an inkling of the transparent nature of "self." Rather than allowing the mind to think about nonessential aspects of past or future, it is preferable to direct the mind toward impermanence in all its aspects.

The arising and ceasing of the breath is easy to observe and understand. The arising and ceasing of the mind as it watches the breath is just as apparent when we observe the fact that there is movement. All movement must arise and cease, and therefore contains irritation, so that unsatisfactoriness becomes an indisputable factor. The unsatisfactoriness of the breath is not so apparent, because we want to live, and we cannot do so without breathing. But in actual fact, constant movement is constant irritation, which is the cause of unsatisfactoriness. There should be no reason for surprise that the world is full of unsatisfactoriness, because within impermanence no total satisfaction can ever be found.

Whether it is an emotion or a sensation, a thought or a reaction, or a physical movement, everything proclaims the character of impermanence. At this stage we become quite interested in our physical movements because they tell the story so eloquently. We cannot walk a single step without arising and ceasing. We cannot lift an arm without arising and ceasing, or get dressed or undressed without it. We can see the proclamation of the true Dhamma in all that we are and all that we do. Seeing this so clearly helps us to overcome doubt, which gives new impetus to the practice. Doubt is like a brake; it holds us back because we worry about the path and the teacher. When there is no longer any doubt, strength and energy are free to forge ahead to open the path to new insights.

Knowledge of comprehension comes as a next step. We investigate the five aggregates of which we are composed: body or movement, mind consisting of feeling, perception, mental formations or thoughts, and sense consciousness. When the process of arising and ceasing has become clear to us, it has given us such a significant insight into ourselves and others that we no longer need to get angry at anybody, because we know that our anger is merely one of the aggregates arising and ceasing. We no longer need to have passionate desires for anyone or anything, because that too is one of the five aggregates arising and ceasing. At this time, the five aggregates assume a prominent role in our consciousness.

First of all, we observe the aggregates in ourselves. What we don't know about ourselves we will never know about anyone else. We know the movement of our breath, of our body—its decay, its aging, its changeability. We know about our feelings, and we investigate them inside and outside the meditative process. As our interest is aroused, it is possible to continue this kind of investigation in meditation for a long time without being distracted.

We try not to be caught again in the solid, compact aspect of ourselves and others but instead constantly investigate the five aggregates. We can see the physical aggregates in all matter around us and observe their constant change. A tree grows, decays, and dies; leaves grow, decay, and die, and so does everything else in existence. The moment of this realization is a very significant one in our progress toward insight.

The knowledge of arising and ceasing then comes to the point in meditation where only the ceasing, the dissolution, is observed. We see only that aspect because our concentration has become more subtle, so that it actually fastens on to the dissolution of the breath, and on to the cessation of each movement of the mind. At this point we may experience terror, because there is nothing one can grasp or hang on to. Everything is falling apart before one's very eyes, and that affects oneself and all that exists. Although now there seems to be solidity, when the meditative concentration has taken hold and insight has been aroused, it is no longer possible to deny dissolution, and that our usual observation is an optical illusion.

If mind and matter were not constantly falling apart, they would remain static forever, which is impossible. All conditions are constantly changing. Having come to that point of realization in meditation and in one's understanding, it is not uncommon for a feeling of terror to take hold. "What am I to do?" There's nothing to hang on to.

QUESTIONS

STUDENT: *We ourselves are the result of craving and ignorance. What about other forms of life—how do they come about?*

AYYA KHEMA: In the same way.

S: *Thank you. I will have to think about that.*

AK: I would suggest that you do not think about it but meditate on it. You don't have to use all the aggregates; any one of them can lead to insight. But before doing that in the meditative process, first try to reach the calm state, because the mind has an entirely different ability when it is tranquil.

S: *I was intrigued when you said that because mind doesn't cooperate with what you like to think, this means that you don't exist. One doesn't exist?*

AK: Not quite. There's no "owner."

S: *There's no owner? Could you see the mind as someone else's? Do you know what I am getting at? I thought it might be a help, but I don't quite know how to use that feeling.*

AK: It's not somebody else's mind. You can look at it and say, "This is an untrained mind; it's just doing what it wants to do. If I had any say in the matter, if I really owned it, it wouldn't be doing this." That may give you an inkling.

S: *That just makes me regret having an untrained mind.*

AK: That's good, because it will encourage you to train the mind.

S: *You said that momentary concentration could bring insight but that it is not enough to gain calm. Is it common in meditation practice for insight to arise?*

AK: It can be, but momentary concentration only brings momentary understanding. However, insights are not lost. When we have gained an insight during our meditation, it may provide enough calm for tranquility to follow.

S: *Does the insight experience fade in our memory?*

AK: Having understood something deeply changes our inner being.

S: *Why isn't insight impermanent and changing?*

AK: It certainly is. But if you know that, that too is an insight.

S: *I don't understand how insight can be permanent, yet at the same time conditioned, because it's not liberation.*

AK: Insight can lead us to the point where liberation follows. But the insights we have discussed are steppingstones. All are necessary in order to reach liberation, because they provide a steady progression of insight. It may come to the point where the progression has reached its end; when that happens, the insights have come to fruition. Once we have gained any one of them, we are not likely to lose them.

S: *I understand from Zen teaching that when the mind is not grasping at something it is closer to resting in its natural nondeluded state. I am curious to know what Theravāda teachings say about that.*

AK: The Buddha said that his is a graduated form of teaching and compared it to the ocean. If you wade into the ocean from the beach, you first get your feet wet. As you go in further, you get wet to the knees, then up to the waist, and finally up to the shoulders. Then you may actually submerge yourself in the water. This describes the path of insight. It's a graduated teaching and not a way of forcing the mind into a mental corner, to let go of all concepts.

S: *If you were to liken all the false conceptions of ego to a tree, so that the branches of the tree were the various false conceptions about the nature of reality, then I would have thought that insight would be like cutting off a branch. Gradually you cut off all the branches, and then finally you chop the whole tree down.*

AK: Insight means that you see this relative reality in a totally new way, where a tree remains a tree, but with a different value system.

S: *I don't understand the difference between matter and mind. Does matter consist of body and the five aggregates?*

AK: One aggregate.

S: *You said we should observe the movement of the mind. Don't the mind aggregates have the three characteristics of existence: impermanence, unsatisfactoriness, and corelessness?*

AK: Yes. Certainly. Movement is impermanence, and because of impermanence, there is unsatisfactoriness and no substance. Movement is irritation and coreless and therefore a source of unsatisfactoriness. First you have to observe reality within in order to have an understood experience.

S: *I think there is no difference between mind and matter, because, for instance, hearing is not separate from sound.*

AK: The mind is the part that understands the sound; the ear only hears it. In order to get rid of the feeling of compactness and solidity, it is necessary to take this compact person apart. That is the way of insight.

S: *Sometimes I can actually hear sound with nothing else happening.*

AK: When it is only a sound, it's a sense contact that has hit the ear. The minute you say, "It is a horn," the mind is working and conceptualizing. The ear can't say, "It is a horn." On the absolute level of truth there would simply be the experience of sound.

⊰⑂14 Disenchantment

Step 9

In this progression of transcendental dependent arising, joy is an indispensable quality for meditation. Joy stems from gratitude and happiness when we realize that we have the good fortune to listen to the true Dhamma. The meditative steps then lead to insight. We can see that the meditative absorptions are preconditions for the attainment of wisdom, because the mind that has become calm and collected is capable of "knowing things as they really are." The discursive, excited, aggressive, worried, problematic mind cannot be still long enough to ponder deeply and realize intuitively. Such a mind is concerned with whatever it contains. Once we become the master of our mind, we will no longer allow the mind to contain negativities.

States of insight are an automatic and natural progression from meditative calm if we follow the Buddha's directives. However, when the mind does not have sufficient concentration ability, or the wish to become absorbed, it can still attain degrees of insight, such as already described. Terror is then a step on the insight path. A totally happy, peaceful, expandable mind will not be able to experience terror, but the mind mostly concerned with insight will experience strong fear. Often the person who experiences this will stop the practice, or may feel that something is wrong with them. They have heard all about these wonderful meditative states in which the mind is completely empty, and yet, all of a sudden, terror arises.

The great gift of the Buddha's teaching lies in the use of analysis, of step-by-step explanations. If we don't know what we are doing, we will not get very far, because we will either turn our back on it or be puzzled and insecure. Terror and fear need to be accepted as a necessary step, because at that point the mind has seen a different reality, namely the dissolution of all that has arisen, whether it concerns mind or matter. No thought can be retained; it disappears. So does the breath, and even the body when we are concentrating deeply. Where am I then? The question may arise: "What am I doing this for? I thought I was going to get happiness out of it; all I am getting is fear." Then the wish to backtrack may enter the mind, back to a far more pleasant reality. But once we have gained insight we cannot step back again; that is not the way out of terror.

After having experienced terror we must investigate that which is being terrorized. We will realize that our fear stems from the fact that we cannot find the person who is trying so hard to get on the spiritual path, to gain insight and liberation. We can't find him or her because all states associated with "me" are dissolving and disappearing. Now we can get a very clear idea of the dangerous aspect of all "formations," meaning all that arises. Everything that is formed, and therefore exists, brings the danger of extinction with it. Not only does everything dissolve and disappear, but we are attached to formations of all sorts, our own and others', and therefore we are constantly open to loss and bereavement.

A house, for instance, is a formation and has an impeding quality, such as is present everywhere. It impedes our thoughts, actions, time, energy, and abilities. Everything that exists has to be looked after, yet it decays and disappears nevertheless.

The impeding element inherent in all forms and formations is associated with a signifying quality. Not only does our body need continual care and attention, but the mind also has to respond to sense contacts and is under constant pressure to keep out of trouble. We say, "I am feeling pressured, tense, or threatened." Naturally the pressure is there because of all the things that confront us through our senses, to which we react constantly. We have all experienced this for years on end, but we always thought we could get out of it somehow by going somewhere else or doing something else. Movement conceals unsatisfactoriness.

But when we see, through insight, the dangerous capacity inherent in all that exists to impede us and to signify the need for judgment and response, terror subsides. We realize that the terror was actually justified, a true experience on the path to liberation. At such times one needs a teacher to help and advise, otherwise the mind may balk at this rigorous uncovering of truth. That is why the Buddha exhorted his followers again and again to go through the meditative absorptions to give the mind a counterbalance of happiness. A calm and joyful mind has no objection to seeing a different kind of reality.

Having seen the dangers inherent in all formations, we realize that there is nothing to be gained by our being here. Consequently, the desire for deliverance arises, which is a most significant point in insight meditation. It occurs because we feel deeply that existence has nothing to offer—although this feeling does not infer a dislike of existence, which would only sap our energy. Up to that point we have consciously or subconsciously thought that existence in one of the higher or *deva* realms would be desirable, something like paradise. Now we realize that all existence is fraught with the same pressures on mind and body.

Desire for deliverance is conjoined with urgency. Urgency is a very important aspect of one's mental makeup; it prevents procrastination. The Buddha often reminded us that life is very uncertain, and death is inevitable. We don't know how long we shall be able to practice. It's not a matter of age; we just have no guarantees. This helps us to be in each moment and let go of past memories and future hopes. Urgency comes from the desire for deliverance, as we take account of the dangers of existence and realize that nothing can be found that provides complete satisfaction, lasting and total fulfillment. We can have momentary pleasure, but by now we have long since seen that momentary pleasure does not satisfy our quest. At this point disenchantment sets in.

Disenchantment (*nibbīdā*) is a combination of knowing the danger inherent in existence and the desire for deliverance. We have realized that pleasant feelings are just as impermanent as unpleasant feelings, even in the meditative absorptions. With disenchantment, we come to a significant point in our practice. This is the last step on the insight path; the next step is the platform from which we can cross to the other shore. At this time we are automatically investigating the three characteristics of impermanence, unsatisfactoriness, and corelessness to see whether they actually apply to everything. It is no longer necessary to point our mind deliberately in that direction, because the mind now reflects consistently. We want to be sure that what we have understood so far is correct.

The mind reflects on all the phenomena it encounters. It may investigate the four primary elements, and it is no longer fooled into believing that the world contains ultimate value, importance, or continuity. The mind is imbued with urgency for deliverance, because it has truly experienced unsatisfactoriness and has understood it. A teacher can be supportive and helpful, but the real work has to be done by the student. This is one of the most fascinating aspects of the Buddha's teaching, namely, that this is a "do it yourself" job. The only things given are a map with signposts and instructions on its use, but we have to travel under our own steam.

Having investigated the three characteristics sufficiently, we naturally come to the understanding that they are a true description of ultimate reality. Everything is of an impermanent nature and therefore cannot be totally fulfilling, or contain a core substance. It is important to find these aspects in ourselves, but we can profitably investigate all that surrounds us.

Our investigation depends on which one of the three aspects we find most interesting. All three are, of course, interconnected and lead to the same goal. A person who has a lot of faith and confidence usually works with impermanence. It is so prominent in the teaching that the confident mind automatically veers toward it. A person with a great deal of concentration usually likes to investigate unsatisfactoriness, and one who is more analytical prefers to delve into corelessness, substancelessness.

To investigate the last of these, our own five aggregates become our working ground (*kammaṭṭhāna*) in meditation as well as in daily living, akin to a workshop. We observe the arising and ceasing of each of the aggregates to see whether we can find an enduring core or substance in either the body or any one of the four aspects of the mind (feeling, perception, mental formations, and sense consciousness). When disenchantment has set in, this investigative procedure becomes of paramount interest. The mind already knows that everything dissolves, but that realization was connected with a great deal of suffering. In its calm state of disenchantment, the mind wants to renew that understanding now. Only when we repeat an inner realization many times will it become part of our own nature. When we come to the same conclusion time and time again—that there is nothing and nobody who owns any of the aggregates, that there is no core, that all is void of substance—we will create this reality in our inner being. Then we can relate to that feeling at any time we wish.

The mind knows whatever it is directed to. When the mind turns to cooking, it will know about cooking; when it is directed toward gardening, it will know only gardening. When the mind turns to the investigation of its own true nature and already possesses some insight, it will know that there is no substance to be found.

In our daily activities, the primary aspect of mind is mindfulness, or bare attention. On the insight path, the mind deals with the intuitive understanding of all phenomena. Our minds need a lot of convincing. The attainment of liberation or freedom is a slow and arduous process, frequently even tedious, and sometimes appears to make no progress at all. At other times, profound insights follow each other so quickly that we would like to step back and say, "Not so fast, I am not quite ready for all this!" But one can't do that, because the practice takes on its own momentum.

Investigation and contemplation can be done at any time—during meditation, while watching the ocean, or even while just walking. Whenever the mind wants to turn to its true nature, it will reflect upon it. I hope your heart was open to these words.

Questions

STUDENT: *What is important in being a monk or a nun in the Buddha's dispensation?*

AYYA KHEMA: A personality that is useful in the marketplace is useless in the monastery. The marketplace personality wants to be right, is aggressive, knows better, achieves, and becomes. That kind of personality will encounter difficulties in human relationships. In a monastery humility is of prime importance. It's one of the principal qualities we need in order to live together. The people who come together in a monastery are all very different and have little in common other than their desire to find a way out of suffering. Most of them are not even quite sure what their suffering is. That suffering is in our own mind is a truth we only discover later. We can constantly learn from one another and need not try to be more clever than others.

Everybody has suffering, and to be able to extend one's love and compassion toward others is an important aspect of togetherness.

In a monastery there are fewer distractions than in lay life, and therefore we know our suffering more intimately. When one has love and compassion in one's heart, then even dreary winters and tedious practice are quite bearable.

Togetherness works if we extend helpfulness toward one another. We all need a support system. The Buddha had the Venerable Ananda as a friend and attendant. That was his support system. It wasn't necessarily an emotional help, but it was certainly physical. People who live together have to support each other. This includes talking honestly about one's difficulties, so that one can live together as a loving family. The emotional support system prevalent in a family should also exist in a monastery.

Respect and politeness are the first steps toward loving-kindness. They are important because they provide an acceptable, graceful manner of dealing with others. Not wanting to be somebody, but learning to be nobody, is the ultimate result of good practice.

❧15 Dispassion and Freedom

STEPS 10-12

WHEN WE EXPERIENCE true disenchantment with all that the world has to offer, it means that there is equanimity. We are no longer revolted by anything, and neither do we see anything as specifically attractive. It all is just as it is. This is the significant step that brings us from disenchantment to dispassion (*virāga*). Passion is *rāga*, and from it derives the English word "rage": not particularly rage as anger, but rage as raging, "being where the action is." Dispassion means the end of that internal raging, which is the opposite of equanimity. Whatever we confront just is and appears neither obnoxious nor enticing. The mind is not pulled toward or away from its center, and it becomes spacious. There is sufficient mental energy to proceed unhampered on the spiritual path, because our ordinary experiences no longer induce strong reactions.

We are quite clear that everything that exists has aspects of unsatisfactoriness: the body, which decays, the mind, which tries to know, understand, and dominate—all are impinging and signifying qualities. Impinging touches our mental process, and signifying results in reactions, because we perceive and judge. Having seen these as sources of unsatisfactoriness and remaining calm, the mind now tries to find that which will be totally fulfilling.

The world, containing no stability, is recognized as an ever-changing phenomenon. Since everything for which conditions are a prerequisite for existence cannot be relied upon (conditions being fragile and changing), it is clear that the search must now be directed toward the unconditioned. The body depends upon the condition of craving, of wanting to be here; so it is born and remains intact, by means of food and drink, until death. The condition of the mind is contacting, otherwise no mental formations arise. None of this is seen as fulfilling, stable, or desirable. Naturally, the mind doesn't know yet what an unconditioned state can be, but it is sharp enough to realize that it needs to turn away from its usual preoccupations. Usually the mind concerns itself with whatever arises, all occurrences being occasions for mental formation.

All that happens has the three characteristics of impermanence, unsatisfactoriness, and corelessness. That body and mind are dependent upon conditions and contain no reality in themselves reveals the ego idea as an illusion. The mind then realizes that there has to be a still point, a point of nonoccurrence, and searches for that complete and utterly peaceful state where nothing arises and nothing ceases.

The mind knows intuitively that a step forward is needed. The nature of this step is well described in *The Path of Purification* (*Visuddhimagga*) by means of an analogy. If one wants to get from one bank of the river, which is worldly life, to the other side, which is liberation, the momentum of practice makes it possible to do so. We tie the rope of materiality to the branch of selfhood, then take hold of the rope, and with the momentum of practice we swing across the river, where we can see the other side. We bend and incline toward the other bank, and let go of the rope of materiality and the branch of selfhood, and drop down on the farther bank. At that moment one has been able to let go of clinging to everything that exists, primarily body and mind. The feeling that there is somebody inside one's body who is "me" has disappeared. In letting go completely, one can drop down onto the opposite bank. Naturally one staggers a little at first, not yet being secure. One has to find one's footing. This is an analogy for the path moment (*magga*) when "change of lineage" occurs. "Change of lineage" means that the person has changed from a worldling (*puthujjana*) to the lineage of the *ariyas*, the noble ones, who have gained enlightenment according to the Buddha's teaching.

The first instance when this happens is called "stream entry" (*sotāpatti*). The "path moment" is a single moment of meditative absorption, with nothing occurring, nothing arising, and therefore nothing ceasing. The path moment, being a single mind moment, does not contain actual recognition. The next two mind moments, which bring freedom (*vimutti*), are the "fruit moments" (*phala*) and signal recognition of one's experience. We can reap the fruit of our practice through this understood experience.

Nonoccurrence means having experienced the unconditioned, where separation is no longer possible. It is a return to the ground of being, to the matrix of existence that is the unconditioned primordial source; out of it arises "being" through craving. For a person who can take that step into the unknown, craving has already abated, and so the unconditioned remains one of the aspects of that person's consciousness.

The experience is a moment in which the "self" notion is obliterated; an enormous sense of relief is felt, as if a great burden has been laid down. That relief is combined with understanding of what has occurred; namely, that consciousness abandoned all that we know, whether beautiful, wholesome, acceptable, or their opposites, and all sense of personal existence was lost.

The impact of the "path and fruit" experience is great, and the mind may now wish to digest it, like taking a rest after a long and strenuous journey through many lifetimes with much suffering. The ability to let go momentarily of our link to the conditioned state has shown us the final resting point. It is only a first step, and there are three more, but this first one is particularly significant and makes an enormous impact on the psyche. Now the mind turns to a review of its own purity and insight, as well as of all the impurities that still exist, so that it can see the path ahead clearly.

The Buddha speaks of ten fetters[8] that bind us to the conditioned state. The first three of these are removed at this point. The most significant one is losing the belief in ourselves as an entity, having identity or personality. The "stream-enterer," one who has taken this first step into joining the ranks of noble ones, is not yet able to maintain a constant inner feeling of "no-self" but will never again believe himself or herself to be a person of solidity, compactness, and core substance. Although the wrong view of self has been lost, this is only a viewpoint and not yet a steady experience, comparable to the "kindergarten class" of enlightenment.

The second fetter that is lost is the belief in rites and rituals. That doesn't mean that one cannot perform them, but their importance and efficacy are shattered. Something entirely different has brought release and relief, namely the letting go of attraction and repulsion, which means absolute nonreaction to feelings. In seeing the futility of trying to find satisfaction in any conditioned state, our former craving and grasping has given way to equanimity. The result is the ability to abandon the personality illusion completely, together with all expectations for oneself. No rite or ritual could accomplish that.

The third fetter that is lost is skeptical doubt (*vicikicchā*). Skeptical doubt and belief in rites and rituals are entirely relinquished. The wrong view of self is eliminated but has not yet given way to a complete nonfeeling of self. Skeptical doubt can no longer impede practice, because the Buddha's words have been proved correct. There is nothing to doubt. One knows from personal experience that consciousness can contain either the cycle of birth and death or liberation and that liberation is possible for a human being. Traditionally, it is said that a stream-enterer has a maximum of seven more lives as a human being before becoming fully enlightened; however, it is possible for liberation to take place in a single lifetime. Such a person will remain the Buddha's disciple and can never again break any of the five precepts.[9]

Although an important step in spiritual emancipation has been taken, greed and hate have not yet been touched. The wrong view of self, which is the root cause for greed and hate, has been corrected, so that they are not quite the same burden that they used to be, but it takes two more enlightenment experiences to eliminate them. From that description alone, we can see that all worldlings are beset by conflicting and disagreeable emotional states. Although these are unpleasant, it is useless to blame oneself or others for them. They are the natural human dilemma, and only when we transcend our humanness and reach supermundane levels of consciousness can we eliminate these problems once and for all.

Once, when the Buddha was sitting under a tree, a wanderer came by, admired his radiant appearance, and asked him, "Are you a god?" The Buddha answered, "No." The wanderer questioned him again: "Are you a man?" The Buddha replied, "No." So the wanderer was puzzled, and said, "Well, what are you, if you are neither god nor man?" The Buddha said, "I'm the Buddha, the Enlightened One, neither god nor man."

The Buddha started life as a human being, just like us. But when the level of the noble ones is reached, a transcendental quality enters, so that the relationship with the human level subtly changes. The stream-enterer has gained a foothold in the family of noble ones.

Dispassion—not being attracted or repelled—means that we can live in the world quite easily. The difficulties we used to encounter when we divided the spiritual life from nonspiritual activities have vanished. When there is no division in the mind, latent energy is set free, and we can use it to let go of all craving for that moment. Some of the cravings reappear for the stream-enterer, but some essential ones are shattered, namely self-assertion, self-importance, and self-appreciation. Letting go of craving primarily refers to letting go of the notion of selfhood, which is the meaning of corelessness, substancelessness, and void.

It does not mean not to have thoughts any more, or to stop functioning in the world. A stream-enterer looks, acts, and talks just as before. Only the viewpoint from which he regards it all is changed completely. It's not just an on-and-off affair of remembering impermanence, but an inner transformation. The human realm needs to be transcended because all human beings live there with delusion, which creates unhappiness. This inner transformation generates a great deal of compassion for beings lost in the wheel of birth and death without guidelines.

The feeling of the fruit moment can be resurrected at any time, and will thereby become part of that person's inner experience, providing ultimate peacefulness. The path moment occurs only once at each of the different stages of enlightenment. Continual practice is necessary in order to be able to take the next step and become a "once-returner" (*sakadāgāmi*).

A once-returner loses none of the remaining fetters; hate and greed are diminished, but not yet eliminated. A once-returner has had a second path and fruit experience, which is easier to establish after having been able to take this enormous leap across the river initially. Since the stream-enterer still experiences unsatisfactoriness, knowing that there is a state of being without unsatisfactoriness gives strong impetus to go further. A stream-enterer therefore knows that it is necessary to turn the mind away from worldly affairs, because they are a disturbance. The mind needs to have such a direction as its determining factor.

Only the enlightened one, who has completed the task, is no longer affected by the world. His mind can never be shaken again. Anyone who is still on the path to liberation will seek solitude at times for intensive practice. One needs to revive the fruit moment consciousness through concentrated meditation and by turning one's mind away from mental occurrences, in the realization that this is peace and fulfillment. Our consciousness yearns for the still point, and the more often one enters into it, the easier it becomes to repeat. When there is no mental movement at all, we can let go again to release ourselves from existence. Then we realize that we have arrived exactly where we have always been, except that before, we considered appearances desirable, valuable, and worth continuing.

For most people, this naturally goes against the grain. We need much practice and repetition to be able to turn our mind so completely that we reach that point. If we felt revulsion for existence, that would just be the other side of the coin of attraction. The deep inner conviction that only the unconditioned state is without suffering enables us to reach beyond existence.

It is up to each of us to know which point of our practice we have reached. If we want to follow a road map, we can only do so successfully if we recognize the intersection at which we are standing. The same applies to our spiritual growth when we wish to follow the Buddha's directions.

It is only possible to have a path moment when there is a total letting go. Although the notion of "self" is fully eliminated only for the enlightened one, it is progressively lessened at each path moment. But the meditator's viewpoint is now utterly altered. The ordinary person thinks, "This is me, and I want to become enlightened." Such a view is no longer possible. The meditator who has attained the first and second path moments does not yet have the totality of the "nonself" feeling, although he already recognizes that there is nothing anywhere of real significance.

The "signless liberation" is the goal that is reached by the person who investigates impermanence as the principal subject and finds nothing of a permanent nature anywhere. The "wishless liberation" is available to the person who uses unsatisfactoriness as the primary object of investigation, having understood that unsatisfactoriness cannot arise when there are no wishes. The "voidness liberation" is the doorway for the one who takes "no-self" (*anattā*) as the main subject and finds "self" void of substance.

At that point there are still seven fetters to be lost. The next path moment creates the "nonreturner" (*anāgāmi*), who will not come back to the human realm to reach final liberation. The nonreturner loses the fetters of hate and greed, and although this is a very big step toward liberation, five fetters still remain. The nonreturner has seen reality for what it really is, and is no longer deceived by outward appearances, which designate man, woman, beautiful, ugly, and so forth. All these appearances have fooled us for so long and have constantly resurrected our suffering. Suffering is not only pain, grief, and lamentation, but it is also unsatisfactoriness and nonfulfillment, which we have all known for so long. We can liken the nonreturner's experience to one of those little bubbles we spoke of earlier, that rose out of the matrix of existence and now no longer thinks of itself as a separate bubble; it just sinks back down into the ground of being without any resistance. It no longer wants to be a separate, big, intelligent bubble.

The resurrection of the third fruit moment makes it possible to rest completely within the unconditioned state, which provides a strong shield against suffering, in spite of the existence of the remaining five fetters. The most significant fetter still to be dealt with is ignorance, of which it has been said, "Just as its perfume clings to a flower, so the notion of self clings to the nonreturner."

In reviewing what has happened, the nonreturner becomes aware of this ignorance. If we have some interesting experience in life, we would usually review it later to understand it better. The impact of a path moment prompts such a review. We recapitulate the experience of the fruit moment and check up on the defilements that are eliminated and those that still occur; we also review the liberative experience. This review is undertaken some time after path and fruit have occurred, because otherwise we cannot be sure which impurities still exist. In a once-returner, hate can still be present as irritation and greed as preference, but the nonreturner has none of these left. The attractions of the world no longer tempt him, and unpleasant situations, which confronted even the Buddha, have no repercussions.

Another one of the five remaining fetters is restlessness. Because the notion of "self" has not been totally eliminated, there is still the push to go somewhere else, to do and get something better, with which every worldling is familiar. Restlessness exists in a subtle way. Two further obstacles still have to be dealt with: a desire to be reborn, either in the *deva* or the *brahma* realms, which are the fine-material and the nonmaterial realms. Because there is still an element of clinging to "self," the thought arises that "I" could have a pleasant further existence in one of those lovely realms where there is no suffering.

The fifth fetter is conceit (*māna*), which doesn't mean that a person is conceited, but rather that he or she still conceives of a selfhood. The review would have shown that these fetters still exist. Although the experience of liberation cuts out all notion of selfhood at the time, it still recurs, which shows us how firmly the idea of self is embedded in human beings; even after three liberative experiences, it is still not totally eliminated.

The last five fetters are only lost with enlightenment. To become enlightened, one takes the fourth opportunity to experience path and fruit. No more reviews are necessary, because all defilements have disappeared; there is no aversion, revulsion, or grasping. That is only possible because such a person has completely eliminated the feeling of being "somebody."

The nonreturner works on the five remaining fetters and, having pared them down to the barest minimum, is able to enter into the final path moment. Each path moment, although similar, becomes deeper and more far-reaching, as if we were taking more and more difficult examinations at university and gradually reaching a deeper understanding of our chosen subject. A profound impact is made on the psyche, so that the enlightened consciousness can never return to an ordinary level. Although an enlightened one could live quite an ordinary life, he or she would be constantly aware that only the five aggregates were operating, without any "me" or "mine" feeling related to mind and body. The ever-recurring refrain when anyone mentioned liberation to the Buddha was "Destroyed is birth, the holy life has been lived, what had to be done has been done, there is nothing more to come," which is the traditional formula for confirming the enlightened state.

QUESTIONS

STUDENT: *It's hard for me to trust the aspect of mind that just wants to travel under its own steam toward concentration and liberation, and I felt quite terrified at the sense of dissolution I experienced.*

AYYA KHEMA: As long as we are not enlightened ones there is an ego. The ego is the notion that this is "my" mind. The mind, and the person who thinks they own the mind, would like to have peace. That's a perfectly valid aspiration. The mind knows very well that it needs to stop thinking to attain that goal. If that were something unnatural, it would not be peaceful and wholesome but would lead to agitation and anxiety.

When you experience dissolution and the mind is not happy and at ease, naturally you feel terror. The ego says, "I don't want to be dissolved, I want to be happy; that's what I am doing all this work for." A distinct dichotomy of thinking follows: "I want to become happy, but I'm having knee pains and I am going to pieces. I don't like this at all!" There are two ways of dealing with this. One is that the mind is able to enter into meditative absorptions, terror never arises, and the mind attains insight in a gentler manner. The other way to deal with terror is to know that the fear is valid. This is the point of departure from remaining ego-bound, to seeing that all formations are dangerous, that one cannot find satisfaction in anything that exists.

S: *Do you then choose the ego's reaction of being terrorized as a subject of contemplation?*

AK: You could not help but focus on that feeling, because of its strength.

S: *It's almost as if there are always bubbles coming out of the ground of existence. Why does that have to happen?*

AK: Your question goes back to first causes, one of the four things the Buddha didn't answer. They are called "the four imponderables."

S: *The questions that do not tend to edification?*

AK: Yes, that's right. There are four imponderables, namely, the influence of a buddha, of a person in meditative absorption, the origin of the universe (or humanity), and the intricacies of karma. Questions concerning these are not conducive to practice, and the Buddha said that answers to such questions would only confuse us further. There is no first cause; everything moves in circles.

S: *It appears to me that although we are so anxious to escape from suffering, when suffering ultimately ends, there's nobody at home to enjoy its absence.*

AK: That's right; but peace is established.

S: *What is ego?*

AK: Public enemy number one. There is no other enemy; we all carry the fiend within us. But we also carry wholeness and peacefulness within. We can't separate ego from anything we think or do because all our volition is ego-saturated, like a saturated sponge in which we can't distinguish the water from the sponge itself.

S: *You talked about compassion along with insight. Wouldn't teaching be an aspect of compassion?*

AK: Certainly. Without compassion it would not reach anyone. The Buddha taught every day, even when he was sick, for forty-five years, out of his great compassion for suffering mankind. He wanted to show everyone how to reach the end of suffering, and to teach them a pathway to freedom. The four noble truths are the essence of the Buddha's teaching. They arise intuitively in the mind at the path moment. A buddha understands them without having had a teacher, but for those following the Buddha's path, they are realized because they have become part of one's mind continuum through the teaching. This occurrence is likened to the sun coming up, so that light is shed, darkness is dispelled, warmth is provided, and cold eliminated. We can see objects clearly because the darkness has gone, and we can feel secure, warm and safe because coldness has been removed. The same happens with the four noble truths: they arise in the mind spontaneously because the third noble truth of liberation is the sun, which shines light into the mind and warmth into the heart. One who has reached liberation is a person who has become the Noble Eightfold Path.[10]

✺16 Day by Day

THERE IS A PROPHECY in the commentaries that predicts that after the Buddha's *parinibbāna*, the Dhamma will last for five thousand years, and the words *anicca*, *dukkha*, and *anattā* will not be heard again until the next buddha arises, which may be eons away. The next buddha is to be named Maitreya Buddha, from the Sanskrit *maitri*, meaning loving-kindness. However, in the middle of those five thousand years there will be a period of one hundred years during which the Dhamma takes an enormous upswing. We are at the moment in the thirty-third year of these hundred years, and the Dhamma is reaching the Western world as never before. This is the first time in the history of mankind that Tibetan teachers have come out of Tibet and are bringing Buddhism to other countries—even to India, the country of its origin, where Buddhism had almost died out. This is, then, a time when we have a unique opportunity to gain enlightenment, and we should not waste our lives on nonessentials. The Dhamma is available to us now and may not be so available in the future.

Let us therefore take a look at how we can use what we have heard or experienced of the Buddha's teaching. We cannot separate meditation from living. Unless the two are joined together, we will find it difficult to make spiritual progress; we will feel torn between priorities, not knowing where we belong. We have to integrate our activities into one whole. To be "holy" means to be whole; we can learn to use our spiritual practices in all the circumstances of our lives.

We need a clear direction as to what we want in life. It helps to write down whatever comes to mind and then cross out what is not pertinent. Make a list of priorities, and check it after a few days to see if you still feel the same way. The list changes again and again, and one day there may be nothing left on it but liberation. When that happens, you will have recognized the urgency. Up to that point, priorities keep changing and a multitude of things will come and go. In the beginning there may be, "I want some peace and happiness," or "I want more friends," or "I want more free time." But if you examine the list closely, in the end it comes down to one thing only: "I want to get rid of my suffering." If you believe the Buddha's words, then the only thing worth aiming for is liberation. In that case, let us have a look at what the seven factors of enlightenment can do for us.

The seven factors of enlightenment are called *bojjhanga* in Pali. *Bodhi* means enlightenment, and *anga* denotes limbs, like arms and legs. So they are the seven limbs of enlightenment.

Mindfulness takes pride of place, being the first on the list. That doesn't mean that the other factors are less important, but without the first one there can be no entry into practice. The importance of the doorway of mindfulness should never be underestimated. It contains all the spiritual qualities we need in daily life.

What is mindfulness, and what can it do for us? There are four foundations or bases, of which the first one is the body (*kāyânupassanā*). That seems simple and straightforward, yet the Buddha said, "Who does not have mindfulness for the body does not enter into the deathless realm." We all know that we couldn't possibly be this body; we have to be more than that, yet we identify ourselves with it. We look in the mirror and say, "I am not looking very well. I'd better do something for myself."

Mindfulness has both mundane and spiritual applications. The mundane application helps us to watch what we are doing, so that we can avoid using the body in a wrong or harmful way, such as breaking any of the precepts, or harming anyone physically. Mindfulness of the body helps us to act harmoniously, easily, and efficiently in every aspect of everyday life. In watching our bodily actions, we can preserve our energy for essentials. Otherwise, because of our innate restlessness, we would often use the body needlessly.

The spiritual application of mindfulness can already be found in the word itself. The "mind" is "full" of what is actually happening. When we keep our attention on our own body, we can become aware of its real nature of constant movement. Even in deep sleep the body alters its position to ease discomfort. Subconsciously the mind is aware of the pain in the body, and when we wake up in the morning we cannot even count the number of times we have moved in our sleep. The movement induced by discomfort also is the movement of impermanence. Everything in the body has to move—breath, heart, blood, cells—otherwise we would die. Awareness of constant movement is an important insight. The spiritual aspect of mindfulness transcends the mundane, utilitarian application and recognizes the body not as solid but as having the nature of constant change. We can know this intellectually, but we need to imbibe it experientially. The mind knows and is aware, and the body is its unwilling servant. If there were a body without a mind, we could cut it up and it would not object. It is just made up of bones, flesh, blood, guts, and all its other parts. But if it is inhabited by a mind, we have a totally different situation. This gives us an important clue into mindful living and insight into reality.

The second foundation of mindfulness is our feelings, that is, sensations and emotions. If we have a visual mind, sometimes emotions appear as pictures. If we have a verbal mind, they may appear in the form of a story. To be in touch with one's feelings is of primary importance. We mustn't be split between head and heart. It is essential for everyone, independent of their lifestyle, to recognize their emotions, because this is where the action lies. Our emotions are our point of departure. In the worldly dependent arising, the doorway out of the wheel of birth and death is explained to be between feelings and craving, wanting or not wanting, which is the reaction to our feelings.

In the meditative process we have to get in touch with our feelings, otherwise meditation remains an intellectual creation and does not become an understood experience. Life has to be experienced, not thought about. When we try to think about life, we conjure up past and future. The present, this moment, has to be known as an experience, and that will always involve our feelings. We constantly react to them, whether we are aware of it or not. Our feelings result from our mind contacts through the six senses, which take place continually in the waking state. If we do not use mindful awareness, our reactions could often be unwholesome or hurtful for ourselves and others. If we are unaware, we can't effect any changes. The formula is "Recognition, no blame, change." This formula is useful every time our emotional life becomes dark and heavy, with feelings of depression, aversion, or unhappiness arising. We don't have to allow these feelings to remain and continue, thereby being the victim of our emotions.

Only when we become master of our emotions do we have a chance to live peacefully and harmoniously. From being the victim to becoming the master, there are steps we can take to bring us nearer to our goal. The first step is recognition, and understanding that no blame attaches to our reactions and that change is possible. Unless we gain insight into ourselves through mindfulness, our reactions will remain more or less preprogrammed. We have been responding to the same triggers in the same way, over and over again.

Sometimes we can recognize such a "trigger" if, for instance, somebody says something totally innocuous, yet we react badly. Five minutes later we might realize that the person resembles somebody we dislike, and so we become aware of an old program being replayed: we are reacting to an unpleasant feeling produced by sight contact. At other times we might react to unpleasant feelings produced by sound contact. Somebody may say something that seems unacceptable to us. A little later we might realize that it sounded similar to a teacher we once had in school, whom we disliked. What was said was probably perfectly legitimate, but our program responded unfavorably.

This means getting in touch with our feelings and understanding them better. Some are pleasant, some are unpleasant, some are neutral, but our reactions don't have to be preplanned, impulsive, instinctive. We can look at them with mindfulness and put the brakes on. Substitution is much easier than just dropping what is in the mind. Although dropping is the perfect way to get rid of clinging, it is more difficult because it is a letting go aspect. In the beginning, substitution is a necessary response.

The first recognition has to be that the trigger for our reactions is outside and the reaction is inside. We can determine what we are going to deal with. "Am I going to attend to the trigger, or to my inner life?" If we have any sense, we will deal with our own reactions. Triggers are so multitudinous in this world that it's impossible to get rid of all of them. We have a greater chance of success if we deal with what is happening inside us.

When aversion, rejection, resistance, anger, jealousy, pride, greed, or craving arise within, we can take a moment to look at them mindfully. When we recognize their burdensome impact on us, we understand that we need not continue to let them exist. We can substitute compassion, or the idea that they are not important, or the understanding of impermanence, or corelessness. This is particularly true of anger, which makes life so very unpleasant for oneself and others. When we get angry with a person, we can ask ourselves first of all, "What am I getting angry at? Is it the hair, the nose, the eyes, or what? Am I getting angry at his words?" If it is really unpleasant speech, it means the other person is unhappy. "Why should I get angry, then? Why can't I be compassionate?" If we can change our anger to compassion, we will feel good, the other person will feel good, and we will have taken a step forward on our spiritual path.

If we blame ourselves for our negative reactions, we are also apt to blame others. Recognition of the emotion, acceptance of the fact that "this one got away," and determination to try again are all that is possible and useful. There are going to be many emotions that will "get away" before we master them—not only anger, but also greed. We've been reacting for many lifetimes and this may be the first time we are trying to stem the flood. That makes all the difference.

We could say that feelings are the most important aspects in our inner life, that our inner life depends on them. If our inner life is smooth and harmonious, our outer life will follow suit.

Once we have been roused to anger and have been able to transform it into compassion, we are imbued with confidence that we can do this again, which gives new impetus to our practice.

Our thoughts, the process of thinking, form the third foundation of mindfulness. We have to be able to differentiate between thinking, experiencing, and feeling. If we are aware of our thoughts, we can choose between daydreaming and directional thinking, as in contemplation. Our escape route from suffering is often thinking, and if we haven't realized that, we might even consider it effective. But as a matter of fact, thinking is actually suffering. Its constant movement is irritating and usually produces no results. Thinking only becomes useful when it creates an understood experience.

The fourth foundation of mindfulness is the content of our thoughts. We don't allow thoughts to happen, but we observe what is going on in our mind as they come. An unwholesome thought is often preceded by unpleasant, ominous feelings, and sometimes by fogginess, anxiety, or irritation. An unwholesome thought throws its shadow ahead, as if to say,

"I'm coming, watch out!" Unwholesome thoughts are energy consumers without a source of regeneration.

The Buddha gave five guidelines on how to combat unwholesome thoughts. The first method is substitution, just as we do in meditation. He compared it to a wedge that a carpenter uses to plug a hole; when the carpenter finds it doesn't fit, he carefully extracts it and substitutes a more appropriate one.

The second method is through shame and disgust. The Buddha compared it with a young couple, dressed in all their finery, who go out into the street and suddenly realize that each is carrying the carcass of a dead animal around their neck. They hurriedly go back into their house, clean themselves, and change clothes before they go out once again. This is our recognition that our unwholesome thoughts give us a dirty and unpleasant appearance, so that we change them quickly.

The third method shifts the focus of our attention. The Buddha compared it with meeting an acquaintance with whom we don't want to become involved; we do not greet him or engage him in conversation but carry on with our tasks as if we hadn't seen him. This means we don't involve ourselves with our unwholesome thoughts but keep our attention on something productive.

The fourth method is recognition of discomfort. The Buddha uses an analogy of a man who is running and who realizes that he feels very uncomfortable, so he starts walking instead. He still feels ill at ease, and stands still. After a while that too is bothersome, so he sits down. When that too becomes tiring, he lies down and finally feels really comfortable. This applies to our recognition that our unwholesome thoughts give us discomfort and make us feel ill at ease, so we gradually change from negative to neutral to positive thinking.

The fifth method is suppression. Anything is better than unwholesome thoughts. The Buddha compared it to a big strong man taking a small weak one by the neck and drowning him. It is better to drown our unwholesome thoughts, either by diversion or suppression, than carry them with us to an undoubtedly unpleasant ending.

The recognition of unwholesome thoughts and reactions is rather like a questionnaire. "Why should this make me angry?" Each answer requires a new question until we reach the bottom line, which is always "ego." It is not useful to say, "It's just my ego," and leave it at that. We have to reach that conclusion through our own introspection.

The triggers in the world exist for one reason only: to show us what we need to learn. We should have a feeling of gratitude toward our difficulties because they are our teachers. If we can accept our whole life as nothing but an adult education class, then we have the right attitude. If we are looking for pleasure and comfort, we will have one disappointment after another.

Mindfulness needs the companionship of clear comprehension. Mindfulness knows, but clear comprehension understands, using four aspects. The first one is the purpose of our thought, speech, or action. After we have ascertained that the purpose is useful, we consider the next step, deciding whether we have skillful means in mind. Then we check whether purpose and means are within the Dhamma, that is, wholesome; no end can justify bad means. Having completed the thought, speech, or action, we inquire whether our purpose has been accomplished, and if not, why not. If it hasn't been accomplished, the answer may lie in unskillful means. There is no reason why, from the very onset of our practice, we should always be successful, but we can learn from each experience.

The first and second verses of the *Dhammapada* say:

> Mind is the master.
> If one thinks with an unwholesome mind,
> unhappiness will follow one,
> like the wheel follows the hoof of the ox.
> If one thinks with a wholesome mind,
> happiness will follow like one's shadow.

The second of the seven factors of enlightenment is the investigation of Dhamma. This can be looked at in two ways. The investigation of Dhamma can mean, in the first place, knowing the teaching—not just the words, but also the meaning. A verse in the *Dhammapada* illustrates this:

> Far better to know one single line
> that one can actually manifest,
> than to know a thousand useless lines.

Knowing little and being able to live accordingly is far more useful than knowing a great deal and being unable to act upon any of it. We can investigate the Dhamma in such a way that we understand it and make it our own through practice, which is the source of wisdom.

There is a second meaning to the Pali word *dhamma*, and that is "phenomena." Here we investigate everything we see, hear, touch, taste, smell, think, and feel as being impermanent, unsatisfactory, and coreless. We usually find that we prefer one of these three as our main subject of contemplation. This investigation and contemplation should not be limited to meditation courses, but it can become a meditative habit in daily life. Each one of the three characteristics, when penetrated and fully realized, leads to the same insight-wisdom.

The third enlightenment factor is energy, which is both physical and mental. The latter consists of volition and determination, the physical being very much influenced by the mind. If our mental energy is one-pointed, and we know exactly what we want to do and where we are going, we will find that our physical energy will be greatly enhanced. Everybody has physical limitations, but mental energy is the deciding factor. If we have a one-pointed direction and know the obstacles on our way are of our own making, then we will not let them deter us. Our obstacles are our challenges to arouse more energy. Energy provides and sustains effort, which we need to learn to balance, like walking on a tightrope. If we tighten up too much, we will tumble down one side. If we let go too much, we will fall down the other side. If we realize that our strength is being depleted to the point where we can no longer focus, we know we have done too much. If we realize that we have been looking for comfort and pleasure, we know we haven't done enough and have to find the middle way again.

The next four of the seven factors of enlightenment are qualities of the four meditative absorptions. They start with rapture and end with equanimity. Equanimity is a feature of the fourth meditative absorption, but it is also a state of mind that comes with insight. It enables us to jump across to the other bank, as discussed earlier, namely, equanimity about all formations, about everything that exists.

All the factors of enlightenment are inherent in us and can be cultivated and perfected. We all have some mindfulness; we can investigate the

Dhamma, have energy, and are able to meditate with some peacefulness. We have the potential within us, but these qualities only become enlightenment factors when we can perfect them in order to make the enormous leap from worldling to noble one. All seven factors are within our capacity to practice in daily life if we continue to meditate, study, investigate, and contemplate. This will provide us with a guideline, a direction for our life.

A good spiritual friend who will help us to stay on the path, with whom we can discuss our difficulties frankly, sure of a compassionate response, provides an important support system that is often lacking. Although people live and practice together, one-upmanship often comes between them. A really good friend is like a mountain guide. The spiritual path is like climbing a mountain: we don't really know what we will find at the summit. We have only heard that it is beautiful, everybody is happy there, the view is magnificent, and the air unpolluted. If we have a guide who has already climbed the mountain, he can help us avoid falling into a crevasse, or slipping on loose stones, or getting off the path. The one common antidote for all our hindrances is noble friends and noble conversations, which are health food for the mind.

Questions

STUDENT: *How can I eliminate sloth and torpor in daily living?*

AYYA KHEMA: If sloth and torpor arise in daily life, it's usually due to ill will. For ill will we need the substitution of opposites, namely, loving-kindness for oneself and others. We also need to remind ourselves that the past is irrevocably gone, the future just a concept, a hope, and that we have only this one moment in which to realize our aspirations.

S: *Is it all right to pat oneself on the back mentally if a wholesome thought or feeling arises?*

AK: Certainly. Who would do it for us otherwise? It doesn't mean we become self-satisfied, only contented.

S: *Could you please expand on ill will, and say a little more about it?*

AK: Ill will is just another expression for anger, or hatred. We can call it aversion, resistance, rejection, fear, jealousy, or envy—all these belong under the same heading.

S: *Could any of these emotions ever be justified?*

AK: Everybody tries to justify them, but nobody succeeds. All of these are such very unpleasant emotions that the one who has the emotion suffers most. We can justify them as much as we like, but that doesn't change their unpleasant impact. In order to grow spiritually, we need to understand that a trigger has generated a reaction, indicating to us that this emotion is one of the weeds growing in our heart, which we need to attend to.

PEMA CHÖDRÖN: *Ayya Khema, I want to take this opportunity to thank you. I told you that in my early conversations with Trungpa Rinpoche, he has said to let it be known that the vision of this monastery [Gampo Abbey] was to admit all schools of Buddhism as well as contemplative traditions of all religions; to welcome them there to preserve their own traditions purely, so that there could be a sharing of each other's insights. In this way, we would undercut sectarianism, narrow views, and chauvinism of any kind, without in any way diminishing the purity and power of each tradition.*

May all beings be happy.

❧ Notes

1. At his enlightenment, the Buddha proclaimed the four noble truths: (1) the noble truth of unsatisfactoriness; (2) the noble truth of the origin of unsatisfactoriness (which is craving); (3) the noble truth of the final extinction of unsatisfactoriness (which is liberation); (4) the noble truth of the path leading to the final extinction of unsatisfactoriness (which is the Noble Eightfold Path).

2. The two teachings are on worldly dependent arising (discussed in this chapter) and transcendental dependent arising (discussed in the remainder of the book, beginning with chapter 5).

3. The other three imponderables are: (1) the intricacies of karma; (2) the range of influence of a buddha; and (3) the range of influence of a person in meditative absorption. See also pp. 178-80

4. (1) Mindfulness, (2) investigation of the law (of nature), (3) energy, (4) rapture, (5) tranquility, (6) concentration, and (7) equanimity.

5. *Ficus religiosa*, a species of fig tree, named bodhi, "enlightenment," since it sheltered the Buddha during his enlightenment struggle.

6. The five aggregates making up a human being: body, feeling, perception, mental formations, and consciousness.

7. (1) Generosity, (2) moral conduct, (3) renunciation, (4) wisdom, (5) energy, (6) patience, (7) truthfulness, (8) determination, (9) loving-kindness, and (10) equanimity.

8. (1) Personality belief (wrong view of self), (2) skeptical doubt, (3) belief in rites and rituals, (4) sensual desire, (5) ill will, (6) craving for fine-material existence, (7) craving for nonmaterial existence, (8) conceit, (9) restlessness, and (10) ignorance.

9. (1) To refrain from killing living beings, (2) to refrain from taking what is not given, (3) to refrain from sexual misconduct, (4) to refrain from lying and harsh words, and (5) to refrain from alcohol and drugs.

10. The fourth noble truth consists of: (1) right view, (2) right aspiration, (3) right speech, (4) right action, (5) right livelihood, (6) right effort, (7) right mindfulness, and (8) right concentration.

❧ Glossary

The following Pali words encompass concepts and levels of ideas for which there are no adequate synonyms in English. The definitions of these terms have been adapted from the Buddhist Dictionary, by Nyanatiloka Mahathera.

anāgāmi The "nonreturner," a noble disciple on the third stage of holiness.

anattā "No-self," corelessness, nonego, egolessness, impersonality; "neither within the bodily and mental phenomena of existence, nor outside of them; can be found in anything that in the ultimate sense could be regarded as a self-existing real ego identity, soul, or any other abiding substance."

anicca "Impermanence," a basic feature of all conditioned phenomena, be they material or mental, coarse or subtle, one's own or external.

arahant The enlightened or holy one. Through the extinction of all defilements, he or she reaches in this lifetime the deliverance of mind, the deliverance through wisdom, which is free from defilements, and which he himself has understood and realized.

ariya Noble ones; noble persons.

avijjā Ignorance, nescience, unknowing; synonymous with delusion; the primary root of all evil and suffering in the world, veiling man's mental eyes and preventing him from seeing the true nature of things.

bojjhanga The seven links (limbs, factors) of enlightenment:
  1. Mindfulness
  2. Investigation of the law
  3. Energy

4. Rapture
5. Tranquility
6. Concentration
7. Equanimity

devas Heavenly beings, deities, celestials; beings who live in happy worlds but are not freed from the cycle of existence.

Dhamma The liberating law discovered and proclaimed by the Buddha, summed up in the four noble truths.

dukkha 1. In common usage, "pain," painful feeling, which may be bodily or mental; 2. In Buddhist usage, as, for example, in the four noble truths: suffering, illness, and the unsatisfactory nature and general insecurity of all conditioned phenomena.

jhāna Meditative absorptions; tranquility meditation.

kammaṭṭhāna Literally, "working-ground"; that is, for meditation; the term in the commentaries for subjects of meditation.

karma "Action"; denotes the wholesome and unwholesome volitions and their concomitant mental factors, causing rebirth and shaping the character of beings and thereby their destiny. The term does not signify the result of actions, or the deterministic fate of man.

karunā Compassion, one of the four sublime emotions.

kāyānupassanā Contemplation of the body, one of the four applications of mindfulness.

khandha The five "groups," "heaps," or "aggregates"; the five aspects in which the Buddha has summed up all the physical and mental phenomena of existence, and which appear to the ordinary man as his ego or personality, to wit: body, feeling, perception, mental formations, and consciousness.

lokiya "Mundane"; all those states of consciousness and mental factors arising in the worldling, as well as in the noble one, that are not associated with the supermundane.

lokiya paticca samuppāda Worldly dependent arising; the wheel of twelve causes and effects fueled by ignorance that keeps us trapped in the cycle of birth, death, and rebirth.

lokuttara "Supermundane"; a term for the four paths and four fruitions.

lokuttara paticca samuppāda Transcendental dependent arising; the linear twelve-step series of causes and effects that begins with recognizing unsatisfactoriness and ends with liberation.

maggaphala Path and fruit. First arises the path consciousness, immediately followed by fruition, a moment of supermundane awareness.

māna Conceit, pride; one of the ten fetters binding us to existence, also one of the underlying tendencies.

mettā Loving-kindness, one of the four sublime emotions (*brahmavihāra*).

muditā Altruistic joy (sympathetic joy), one of the four sublime emotions.

nibbāna Literally, "extinction," to cease blowing, to become extinguished. Nibbāna constitutes the highest and ultimate goal of all Buddhist aspirations, that is, the absolute extinction of that life-affirming will manifested as greed, hatred, and delusion, and clinging to existence, thereby the absolute deliverance from all future rebirth.

nibbīdâ Turning away, disenchantment.

nīvarana "Hindrances"; five qualities that are obstacles to the mind, blind our mental vision, and obstruct concentration, to wit: sensual desire, ill will, sloth and torpor, restlessness and worry, and skeptical doubt.

papañca Proliferation; literally, "expansion, diffuseness"; detailed exposition, development, manifoldness, multiplicity, differentiation.

parinibbāna "Full liberation"; a synonym for liberation, commonly used to refer to the death of the Buddha.

pīti Interest, enthusiasm, rapture; comes to full development in the first meditative absorption, and is then one of the seven factors of enlightenment.

puthujjana Literally, "one of the many folk"; worldling, ordinary man, anyone still possessed of all the ten fetters binding them to the round of rebirths.

rāga Greed, craving; a synonym for *lobha* and *tanhā* and thereby one of the unwholesome roots of existence.

sacca Truth, as in the four noble truths.

sakadāgāmi The "once-returner," a noble disciple on the second stage of holiness.

samādhi Concentration; literally, "the being firmly fixed." One-pointedness of mind.

samatha Tranquility, serenity; a synonym for *samādhi* (concentration).

saṃsāra The round of rebirth, literally, "perpetual wandering"; a name by which the sea of life is designated, ever restlessly heaving up and down.

saṃvega The sources of emotion, or a sense of urgency.

Sangha Literally, "congregation"; the name for the community of monks and nuns. As the third of the Three Gems and the Three Refuges, it applies to the community of the noble ones.

sankhāra Most general usage: formations, mental formations, and karma formations. Sometimes bodily functions, or mental functions. Also, anything formed.

sotāpatti Stream-entry, the first attainment in the process of becoming a noble one.

upekkhā Equanimity, an ethical quality, belonging to the wholesome mental formations; also, one of the four sublime emotions and one of the seven factors of enlightenment.

vedanānupassanā Contemplation of feeling, one of the four applications of mindfulness.

vicāra Sustained application. Continued attention to the object (of meditation).

vicikicchā Skeptical doubt, one of the five mental hindrances and one of the three fetters, which disappears forever at stream-entry.

vimutti Deliverance, liberation; two kinds of liberation are described: deliverance through mind and deliverance through wisdom, equivalent to the fruition of enlightenment.

vipassanā Insight into the truth of the impermanence, suffering, and impersonality of all corporal and mental phenomena of existence.

virāga Detachment, freedom from craving, dispassion.

vitakka Initial application. Fixing the consciousness to the object (of meditation).

yathābhūtañāṇadassana Knowledge and vision according to reality; one of eighteen principal kinds of insight.

❧ Index

Note:
· *Italic page numbers indicate glossary definitions.*
· *Page numbers followed by "q" indicate quotations.*
· *Page numbers followed by "(2)" or "(3)" indicate two or three discussions.*

⊱ About the Author

Ayya Khema was born in Berlin in 1923 to Jewish parents. In 1938 she escaped from Germany and was taken to Glasgow, Scotland. Her parents went to China, where Ayya Khema later joined them. With the outbreak of war they were put into a Japanese concentration camp, where her father died.

Ayya Khema later immigrated to the United States. Between 1960 and 1964 she traveled with her husband and son throughout Asia, where she learned meditation. Ten years later she began to teach meditation in Europe, America, and Australia. She was ordained as a Buddhist nun in Sri Lanka in 1979 by Narada Maha Thera.

In 1978 she established a Theravāda forest monastery, near Sydney, Australia, with Phra Khantipalo. In Sri Lanka she set up the International Buddhist Women's Center in Colombo and Parappuduwa Nuns Island.

In 1987 Ayya Khema coordinated the first ever international conference of Buddhist nuns, where H. H. the Dalai Lama was the keynote speaker. In May 1987 she was the first person ever to address the United Nations in New York on the topic of Buddhism.

She served as the spiritual director of Buddha-Haus in Germany, which she established in 1989, until her death, and in June 1997 she founded the first Theravāda monastery in Germany.

Ayya Khema wrote over twenty-five books on meditation and the Buddha's teaching; her work has been translated into more than seven languages. Her *Being Nobody, Going Nowhere* received the Christmas Humphreys Award.

Venerable Ayya Khema died in Germany on November 2, 1997.

☙ About Wisdom Publications

WISDOM PUBLICATIONS is a publisher of classic and contemporary Buddhist books and practical works on mindfulness. Publishing books from all major Buddhist traditions, Wisdom is a nonprofit charitable organization dedicated to cultivating Buddhist voices the world over, advancing critical scholarship, and preserving and sharing Buddhist literary culture.

To learn more about us or to explore our other books, please visit our website at www.wisdompubs.org. You can subscribe to our eNewsletter, request a print catalog, and find out how you can help support Wisdom's mission either online or by writing to:

Wisdom Publications
199 Elm Street
Somerville, Massachusetts 02144 USA

You can also contact us at 617-776-7416 or info@wisdompubs.org.

Wisdom is a 501(c)(3) organization, and donations in support of our mission are tax deductible.

Wisdom Publications is affiliated with the Foundation for the Preservation of the Mahāyāna Tradition (FPMT).